DIY
Embroidered
SHOES

DIY Embroidered Shoes

Landauer Publishing, www.landauerpub.com, is an imprint of Fox Chapel Publishing Company, Inc.

Copyright © 2024 by Melissa Galbraith and Fox Chapel Publishing Company, Inc.

Project Team
Acquisitions Editor: Amelia Johanson
Managing Editor: Gretchen Bacon
Editor: Sherry Vitolo
Designer: Freire Disseny + Comunicació
Indexer: Jay Kreider
Photographer: Melissa Galbraith

ISBN 978-1-63981-098-7
Library of Congress Control Number: 2024943347

To learn more about the other great books from Fox Chapel Publishing, or to find a retailer near you, call toll-free 800-457-9112, send mail to 903 Square Street, Mount Joy, PA 17552, or visit us at www.FoxChapelPublishing.com.

We are always looking for talented authors. To submit an idea, please send a brief inquiry to acquisitions@foxchapelpublishing.com.

Note to Professional Copy Services:
The publisher grants you permission to make up to six copies of any patterns in this book for any customer who purchased this book and states the copies are for personal use.

Printed in the United States of America
First printing

DIY
Embroidered
SHOES

Techniques, Designs,
and Downloadable
Templates to
Personalize
Your Footwear

Melissa Galbraith

Landauer Publishing

44

48

90

60

82

Contents

74

124

Introduction

Since writing my first book, *How to Embroider Texture and Pattern*, I've been slowly embroidering my entire wardrobe. This started as a way to jazz up plain T-shirts, then became more functional. I started mending small holes and covering stains with embroidery. Eventually, I started stitching on hats, bags, and shoes, too. Nothing in my closet was safe from a needle and thread!

I will admit, I didn't immediately fall in love with shoe embroidery. While hand-embroidered shoes are gorgeous, I've always viewed shoes as very functional parts of my wardrobe. Mine are constantly in need of a wash, and I never seem to have a pair I can keep clean for special occasions. Spending hours embroidering something I might get mud all over took a little getting used to. But, after overcoming my fears of ruining embroidered clothes, I started to get more comfortable with wearing my embroidered shoes along with the rest of my embroidered wardrobe. I absolutely love each and every pair!

What I learned as I began embroidering shoes is that you need to approach the process differently from how you'd approach traditional hoop embroidery. The thicker shoe fabric and unusual angles may feel odd at first, but if you work steadily through the steps I've outlined and take a few breaks as needed, you'll find success. Remember: All hand embroidery projects take a bit of time, and shoe embroidery is no exception.

The patterns in this book are inspired by nature. I pulled inspiration from my surroundings in the Pacific Northwest, trips to desert locales, and reminiscing on the Converse I used to doodle on in high school. I hope you have fun customizing your own shoes with the projects and designs in this book.

Happy stitching!

—Melissa

Materials Prep

Ready to get started? This section walks you through necessary materials like types of shoes, thread, and needles, and also covers the basics of transferring embroidery patterns, splitting and knotting the thread, and more. Even if you've embroidered before, you're sure to find helpful tips to make embroidering easier.

Shoes

Canvas or thin fabric shoes are the easiest shoes to embroider, especially those that lace up (you can open them for a bit more room on the inside of the shoe while you work).

The two primary concerns when choosing shoes for embroidery are material and style.

Canvas or thin fabric shoes (think of Converse- or Keds-style shoes) will be the easiest to stitch on. The thinner the fabric, the less resistance your needle and thread will have as you embroider. This isn't to say you can't embroider on thicker fabrics, leather, or shoes with padding, but those materials will be harder on your hands. You'll find more resistance when working the needle and thread through thicker fabrics.

Shoes that open in the front, such as lace-up shoes, will be the easiest shoes to embroider because you will have easy access to the inside of the shoe. This book also has a few projects that use slip-on shoes. These projects are much more challenging because it is harder to get your hand inside the shoe and see

Breaking In Shoes

New shoes are stiffer than shoes that have been worn or broken in, especially in the heel and toe areas. There are a few different techniques to break shoes in—making them easier to stitch on:

- **Bend the shoe so that the toe and heel areas are twisted and squished in different angles and directions.** By working these sections specifically, you'll wear the inner padding down some to make it easier to stitch through. This will also make your shoes a little more comfortable to wear.

- **Wash your shoes.** Most canvas shoes can be thrown in the washer and dryer. A good wash can help wear the fabric a bit, making the shoe material easier to stitch through. Plus, if they're new shoes, this will ensure any additional dyes are removed before stitching.

the stitching on the inside. Additionally, small shoes are challenging as they have tighter spaces to get into and stitch in.

No matter what kind of shoes you start with, please make sure they're clean! The shoes used in this book are all brand new. I found them on Amazon and at my local craft store in the dyeing and needlework sections. Before starting any embroidery project, remove the laces and save them for when you're finished stitching.

Needlebook with embroidery needles and darning needles

Curved needle

Needle gripper

Various bead styles

Thimble

Embroidery thread

Transfer pen and pencil

Thread gloss

Ponderosa Thread Gloss MOJAVE BLEND

Transfer paper

Embroidery scissors

4 SHEETS FEUILLES

D·M·C®

FONDÉE EN 1746

Simply Trace & Stitch! Juste un trait et brodez!

EMBROIDERY TRANSFER PAPER
PAPIER DE TRANSFERT DE BRODERIE
wax free • sans cire

Transferring the Pattern

This part of the embroidery process can often feel daunting, especially if you don't feel like you have strong drawing skills. Thankfully there are a variety of ways to trace and transfer a design.

CARBON PAPER/TRACING PAPER

This method is great if you have a design already printed. Once transferred and stitched, these designs usually wash out like chalk pencils or can be erased. Carbon/tracing paper is available in various colors like black, blue, yellow, and white, making it usable for any color shoe fabric.

1 **Place the colored side of the tracing paper on top of the shoe fabric.**

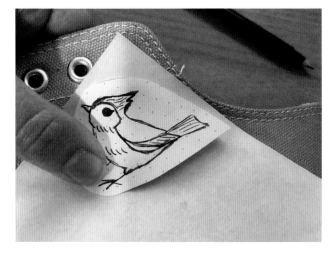

2 **Place the design on top of the tracing paper.**

3 **Using a pen or pencil, trace the design.** Press down hard.

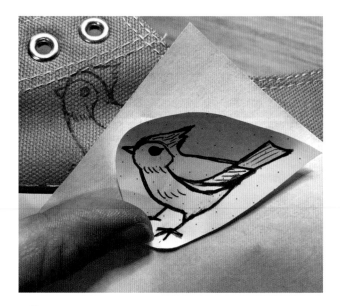

4 **The design is now transferred onto the fabric.**

WATER-SOLUBLE TRANSFER PAPER

This transfer method can be used for any shoe and is most helpful for patterned fabrics. For this transfer method you need to first decide if you're going to print or trace the design. You can print a design directly onto water-soluble transfer paper (I prefer Sulky Sticky Fabri-Solvy because it has a sticky backing) using a printer or trace the design onto the transfer paper.

For this example, I'll trace a drawing from my sketchbook to create the design.

1 **Trace the pattern onto the water-soluble transfer paper.** Use a pen that won't bleed when it gets wet (I like to use a Pilot FriXion Erasable Pen or a pencil). Trim the transfer paper to ¼" (6.4mm) around the edge of the design.

2 **Peel off the backing and press the pattern sticky side down onto the shoe.** Make sure the design lays flat and that there isn't any wrinkled fabric under the design.

> **TIP**
> Cutting the separate parts of the pattern out individually can help you better position the design on your shoe, especially if there are large spaces between the design elements

3 When you're done stitching, simply wash the pattern away with warm or hot water. You may need to agitate the pattern with your finger if there is dense stitching on top of the stabilizer.

TIP

One of the drawbacks of this transfer method is that the sticky backing of the transfer paper can make your needle sticky. To avoid this, just rinse and dry your needle occasionally.

4 Once the stabilizer is washed away, shape the shoe and let it air dry. I like to stuff a small towel in my shoe to help keep its shape as the material dries.

Thread Prep

For most of the projects in this book, you'll use **6-strand embroidery thread**. This means each skein of thread includes six individual strands, so when you cut a length of thread, you will need to split it apart to create the desired thickness. Each pattern details which color to use and how many strands of thread to use in that portion of the pattern.

Clockwise (starting top left): Thread gloss, an embroidery needle threaded with three strands of embroidery floss, and embroidery scissors.

There is a variety of floss types out there, but I encourage beginners to start with the colors I've supplied. Once you're comfortable, then you can experiment!

CUTTING THE THREAD

Those new to embroidery might not realize that cutting the right length of thread makes a big difference! Thread that is too long can get tangled, but having a length that is too short means you'll be constantly threading your needle. Here's a good method for solving that issue.

1 To get started, I flip the skein of thread so that the numbers are at the top. Find the tail end of thread sticking out of the skein top.

2 Hold the skein by your nose and pull out one arm's length of thread. This will give you a consistent measurement without using a ruler or measuring tape.

3 Cut the thread away from the skein. This measurement will be different for everyone. It's the right amount of thread to ensure that the thread is less likely to get tangled. You can always cut the thread a shorter length, but I do not recommend anything longer.

SPLITTING THE THREAD

Many of the projects in this book use a variety of thread weights. Varying the thread weights (1 strand, 3 strands, or even 6 strands) allows you to create different textures and details.

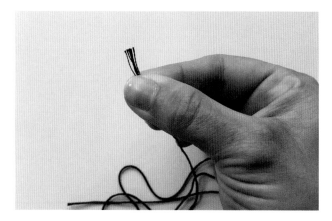

1 **To split the thread apart, pinch the thread between your fingers at one end.** Notice there are six strands.

2 **Gently pull one strand away from the bunch.** Pull straight up and not apart. The thread should bunch under your fingers.

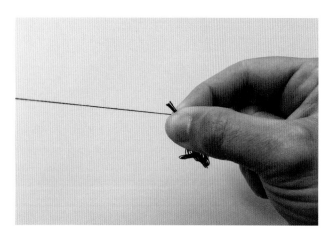

3 **After the one strand is away from the bunch, lay it flat on the table.** Flatten out the thread it was pulled from.

4 **Repeat the process until you have the desired number of strands.** Do not try to pull more than one strand of thread from the bunch at a time. Pulling out multiple strands at a time usually results in a tangled, knotted mess.

TIP

Along with different thread weights, you can also create your own color variations by combining strands from different threads. I've found variegated thread colors to be harder to find and much more expensive than standard cotton embroidery thread. Combining strands from different colors is a simple and inexpensive way to create your own variegated thread options.

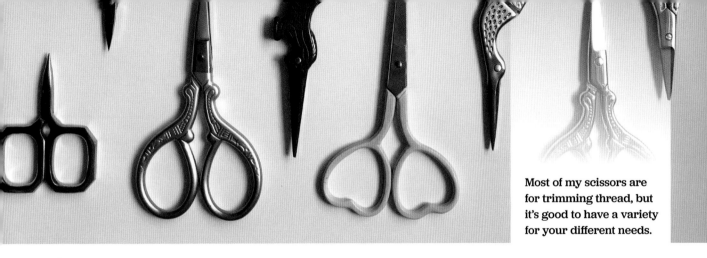

Most of my scissors are for trimming thread, but it's good to have a variety for your different needs.

Scissors

I love collecting scissors. Since starting hand embroidery, finding scissors in bold colors and delightful shapes has been a bonus pastime. You don't need as many pairs as I have pictured, but you'll want at least one reliable pair to use while stitching.

The main thing you need is a **small, sharp pair of scissors** to trim threads. Smaller scissors make it easier to trim thread close to the fabric and get into small spaces, like along seam lines. I recommend finding a pair that fits easily in your fingers and has a longer scissor blade. The longer blade will help you reach more easily into slip-on shoes.

In addition to smaller scissors, you can find **curved scissors**, which have a slightly bowed tip, and **thread snips**, which are often more compact and spring-loaded. These can make it easier to cut threads close to the fabric and reach into tight, curved sections of your shoes.

Needles

Hand sewing needles come in all sorts of varieties. They vary by thickness, length, sharpness, eye size, and more. There are tons of options out there!

For shoes, **darning needles** are the most effective for the thicker fabrics. Darning needles are slightly longer than hand embroidery needles but have a similar eye size. Darning needles are sturdier than embroidery needles because they're designed for mending and stitching through thicker fabrics. The longer length makes it easier to hold the needle while stitching in a shoe.

For slip-on shoes or sections that are narrow or hard to reach into, a **curved needle** is often the best option. These look odd compared to standard hand sewing needles, but the curved needles make it easier to stitch into tight spaces. John James makes a great variety pack of curved needles.

If you don't have darning or curved needles, you can use a hand embroidery needle. The most important thing is to ensure that the needle isn't damaging the fabric when you're stitching through

it. I'd test the needle on the fabric to make sure it doesn't make holes or marks before starting to embroider. As I wrote this book, I tested a variety of needles. Hand embroidery needles tended to bend and break a little easier than darning needles, so keep that in mind if you use one for a project.

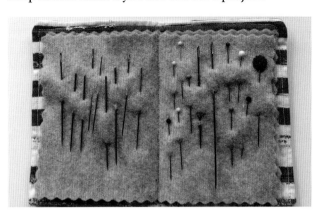

I've built up a large collection of needles. This needlebook is a great way to store needles and pins as well as make it easy for me to find the right one!

THREADING THE NEEDLE

This can often be the trickiest part of embroidery! Here are a few tips to make it easier. And if all else fails, use a needle threader.

1 **After you've split apart the thread (page 14), align all the strands you want to use.** Make sure that the end being threaded through the needle is even. If the thread is frizzy or uneven, trim the edge.

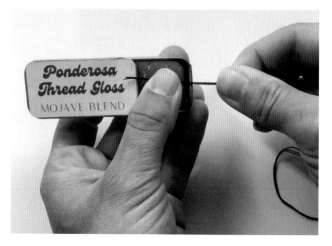

2 **Use thread gloss or get the thread wet so that the strands stick together.** When I first started embroidering, I put the thread ends into my mouth to get them wet and to stick together. Now, I like to use **thread gloss**. This is a scented beeswax mix that acts as a conditioner for the thread. Not only does it help the thread stick together, but it also helps the thread from tangling. And it's easy to use. Simply run the thread across the wax.

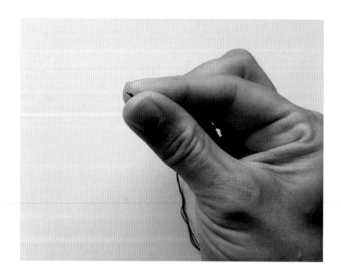

3 **When you're ready to thread the needle, flatten the thread into a straight line.** This will make it easier to fit as you pass the thread through the eye of the needle.

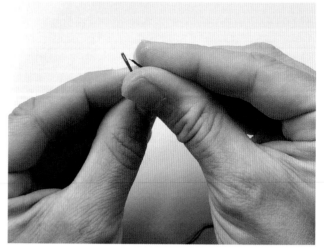

4 **Hold as close as you can to the end of the thread length.** This will help you guide the thread into the eye of the needle without the thread bending or splitting apart.

Grippers and Thimbles

Stitching through some sections of shoes is hard work! Premade shoes are designed to support our feet and make it comfortable to walk around. This also means that shoes have padding and built-in structure. Sections like the heel, toe, around gromets, and where the shoe connects to the sole can all be stiff and harder to embroider.

One thing I found helpful when embroidering in these areas was a **needle gripper**. I found a set that looks like silicone thimbles. After putting them on, I can grip the needle with them and more easily wiggle it through the stiffer fabric. You can find small fabric grips (they just look like little pads of fabric), which can be wrapped around the needle to help move it through the fabric. If you need something sturdier, try using small pliers to pull the needle through the shoe.

I also use a **thimble**. Mine is a vegan-leather thimble with a metal tip. This is the most comfortable thimble, and the metal portion makes it easier to push the needle through the fabric. There are a variety of thimble options available, and you should try a few different types and use the one that works best for you.

Needle grippers and thimbles both help you push your needle through thicker fabrics without as much wear and tear on your hands.

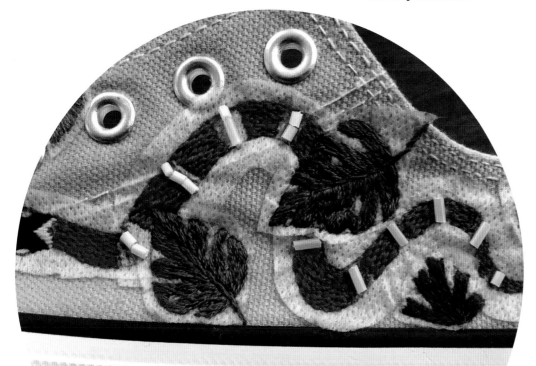

Grippers and thimbles are particularly useful when you need to stitch near seams, eyelets for shoe laces, sole edges, or anywhere that the fabric may be more thickly layered.

Knots

Knots are important for starting and ending a thread when embroidering. This section will cover how to knot the end of your thread to start stitching and how to finish the thread on the back of your embroidery with a knot.

You might notice there are also knots listed in the Stitch Glossary (page 22). These knots, like the French knot, are textural knots that sit on the front of the fabric. The knots detailed in this section will be on the back of the embroidery.

KNOTTING THE END OF THE THREAD

I like to use the **quilter's knot** when knotting the end of my thread. This gives you a solid knot all in one.

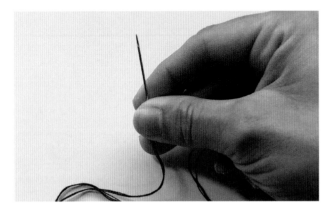

1 **Thread the needle and make sure one side is slightly shorter than the other.**

2 **Hold the needle pointy side up in your dominant hand.** Pinch the very end of the long end of thread in your other hand and cross it in front of the needle, creating a *T* shape with the needle and thread end.

3 **Pinch where the thread and needle cross together between the thumb and finger that's holding the needle.** With your nondominant hand, pinch the thread about 4" (10.2cm) away from the needle.

4 **Use your nondominant hand to wrap the thread around the top of the needle three times.** Tug the thread so it's tightly wrapped.

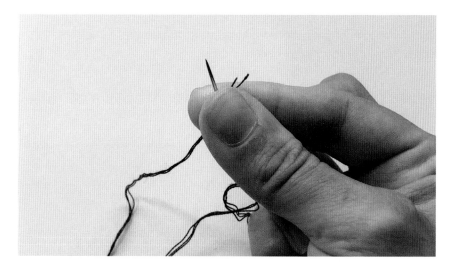

5 Pinch the wrapped thread between the thumb and finger that is holding the needle. Let go of the thread in your other hand.

6 Continue pinching the wrapped thread as you pull the needle straight up. Slide the wrapped thread down the needle and along the length of the thread. Grab the needle at the eye as you pull so that it doesn't come unthreaded.

7 Keep pinching the thread wrap until you get to the end of the thread. This will create a knot. Trim the end of the thread after the knot to ½" (1.3cm).

KNOTTING THE THREAD ON THE EMBROIDERY BACK

There are a couple different knots you can use to end your thread when embroidering. I used to only use a slip knot, but with shoes, some sections are harder to get to than others, making ending the thread a challenge. Because of that, I'm sharing two kinds of knots to help you end your thread.

Slip Knot
For the **slip knot**, I recommend having at least 3" (7.6cm) of thread to work with. The shorter the thread is, the harder it is to create the knot.

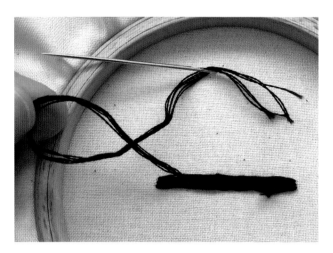

1 Take the thread that's coming out of the embroidery and make a loop.

2 Bring the needle through the loop of thread. Where the thread crosses is going to be the knot. Use your fingers to work the crossed portion of the loop down to be flush with the back of the fabric.

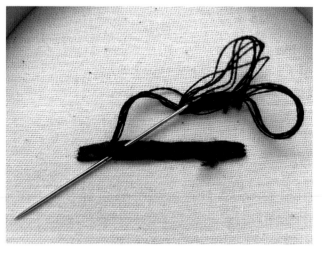

3 Create a knot. When it's flush with the back of the fabric, hold the knot in place with your finger and gently tug the thread end. Cut away the extra thread.

TIP If you are struggling to get the knot flush with the fabric, try holding the loop in place with the point of the needle. As you tug the loop closed, the needle with help guide the knot to the right spot.

4 Use this method if the knot isn't flush with the fabric. Run your threaded needle underneath some of the stitches on the back of the embroidery. This will tug the thread and knot down to the back and protect it from coming undone. Then cut away the thread.

Square Knot

This knot is like tying your shoes. It can be used for short lengths of thread or where you're having trouble reaching the back of the shoe. **Note:** You need at least two strands of thread to create this knot. For sections that are harder to reach, having extra thread to hold onto will make this process easier.

1 **Unthread the needle and unwind the thread so that the thread can be split into two sections.** The sections don't need to be even.

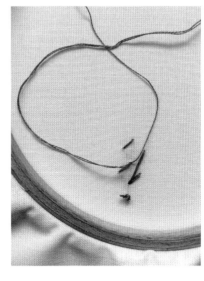

2 **Cross the thread over itself, creating a loop.**

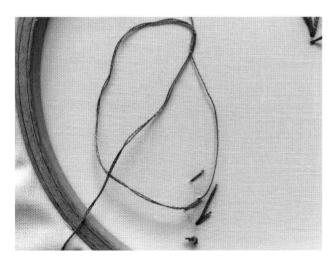

3 **Slide the tail end of the thread in front through the loop.**

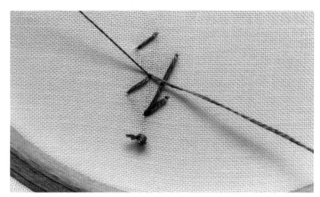

4 **Tug the two ends so that the crossed thread is flush with the fabric.**

5 **Repeat Steps 2 through 4 to secure the knot.** Cut away any excess thread.

TIP

If you are concerned that your knots won't hold tight enough or that your stitching will come undone, add a thin layer of fabric glue to the back of the embroidery on the shoe. I have tried Liquid Stitch and found that it dries clear and is flexible enough for pieces that require movement. I try not to use glue whenever possible, but it can sometimes be helpful and add peace of mind. Before gluing anything, test the glue on a small area of the shoe to ensure it doesn't discolor or ruin the shoe in any way. Once a shoe is glued, you will not be able to adjust any of the stitching.

Stitch Glossary

This section covers the embroidery stitches and variations used in this book. Each stitch creates a unique texture and effect within your design.

BACK STITCH

The back stitch creates short stitches in a row. Like the name suggests, this stitch is made by leaving a space and then going back to fill it in. When the back stitch is used to fill an area, rows are offset like a brick wall.

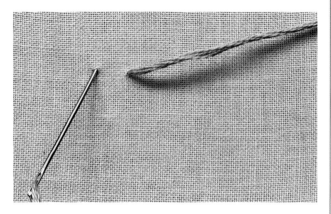

1 **Bring the needle up from the back of the fabric about ⅛"–¼" (3.2–6.4mm) away from the start of the row.** Then bring the needle back down through the fabric where the stitch will end. This creates a single back stitch.

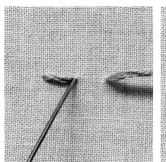 

2 **Add another back stitch to the row.** Leave a space along the row and bring the needle up through the fabric. To connect this back stitch to the last, bring the needle back down through the fabric in the hole of the last stitch.

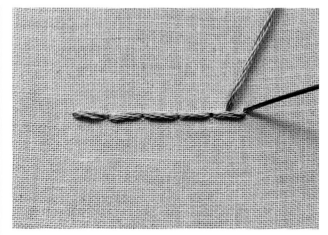

3 **To create a "brick wall" texture, offset each row of back stitches.** Bring the needle up one row above the line of stitches you made. Insert the needle at the middle of the stitch below, then back stitch to the end of the row. Bring the needle up from the back at the middle of the next stitch. Stitch through the first hole in the row. Repeat to create a solid texture.

BEADED BACK STITCH

The beaded back stitch is a great way to attach beads in a line or section.

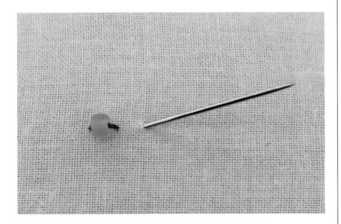

1 **Bring the threaded needle up from the back of the fabric to the front about ⅛"–¼" (3.2–6.4mm) away from the start of the row or the previous stitch.** In the example, I've already made a single beaded back stitch.

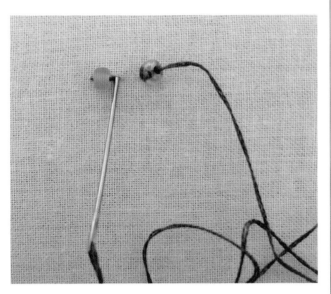

2 **Slide a bead onto the needle and down the thread so that it's flush with that fabric.** Then bring the needle back down through the fabric where the stitch will end (in this example, the hole of the previous stitch). This creates a single beaded back stitch.

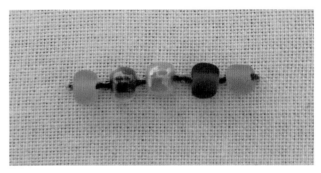

3 Repeat Steps 1 and 2 to continue adding beaded back stitches to the row.

TIP For this stitch, the bead should easily slide down the needle and thread. If it doesn't, switch to a thinner needle (one with a smaller eye) or try using a beading needle.

BEADED SEED STITCH

The beaded seed stitch is a great way to attach beads to fill in sections.

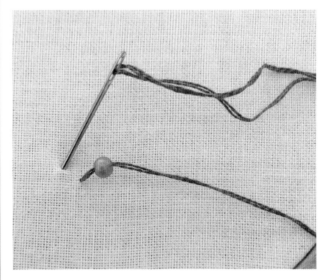

1 **Bring the needle up from the back of the fabric to the front.** Slide a bead onto the needle and down the thread so that it's flush with the fabric. Then make a short stitch in any direction to fill the space.

2 **Leave space away from the previous stitch and bring the needle back up through the fabric.** Slide a bead onto the thread and then make another short stitch in a different direction.

3 **Continue filling the space with short, small stitches that go in different directions.**

TIP
For this stitch, the bead should easily slide down the needle and thread. If it doesn't, switch to a thinner needle (one with a smaller eye) or try using a beading needle.

BERRY STITCH

The berry stitch is two detached chain or lazy daisy stitches (see page 30) made around one other.

1 **Bring your threaded needle from the back of your fabric to the front.** Hold your thread toward the top of the loop being created and bring your needle back down through the fabric right next to where you brought it up.

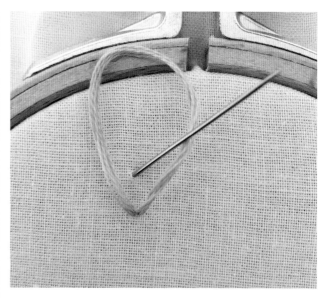

2 **Gently pull the thread until you have a small, open loop on the front of your piece.** Bring your needle up from the back of the fabric to the front, going through the loop. The spot where you bring your needle back up will be where the top of the chain will be formed. Be sure your loop isn't twisted, or the stitch will also be twisted.

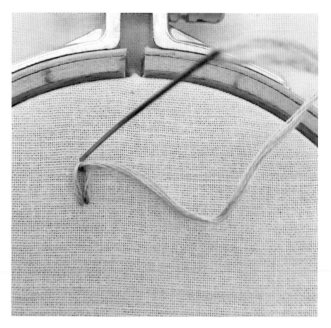

3 **Gently tug the thread through to tight the small loop on the front of your fabric.** To secure the stitch, bring the needle down, back through the fabric on the other side of the top of the loop. This creates a single detached chain/lazy daisy stitch.

4 **Repeat Steps 1 through 3 to create another detached chain/lazy daisy stitch around the outside of the first stitch.** This creates the berry stitch.

BLANKET STITCH

The blanket stitch will be used to attach the soles of the espadrilles to the fabric (see page 121). The example stitches are shown on a flat surface, but each step explains how to use the stitches to complete your shoes.

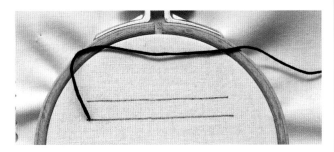

1 **Bring the needle up from inside the shoe through the edge of the sole.**

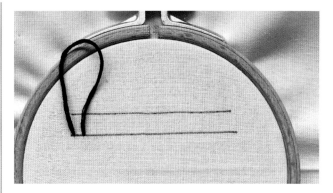

2 **Bring the needle back down into the sole about ⅛" (3.2mm) away from where the thread is coming out.** This will make a loop of thread.

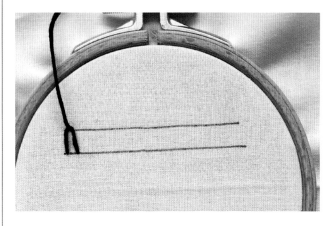

3 **Bring your needle up inside the loop along the edge of the fabric.**

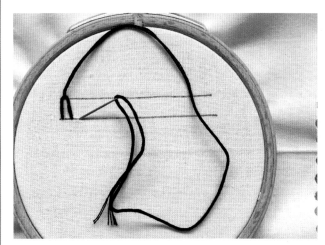

4 **Hold the thread in the direction you are stitching and bring the needle back down through the sole at the bottom point of the blanket stitch.** This will make another loop of thread.

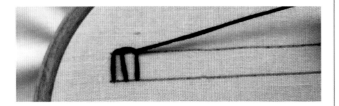

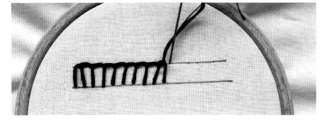

5 Repeat Steps 3 and 4 to continue creating blanket stitches. Make stitches the whole way around the shoe fabric to attach the sole.

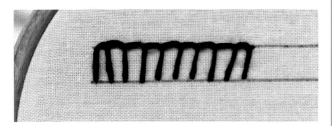

6 To end the blanket stitch, bring the needle back down through the fabric to the right of the top of the last thread loop.

BULLION KNOT

The bullion knot is a long, cylindrical knot. This knot can be used to add a slightly raised texture to a design for leaves, ground texture, and even as flowers.

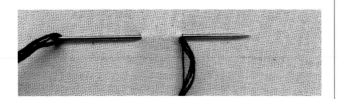

1 Bring the needle up from the back of the fabric to the front. Choose the length of the bullion knot you wish to create and bring the needle back down through the fabric. Before pushing the needle all the way through the fabric, bring it back up next to where the thread is coming out of the fabric.

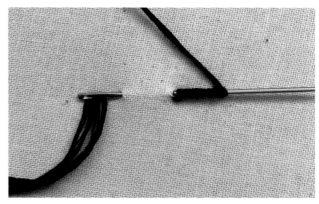

2 With the needle in the fabric, wrap the thread around the needle. The length of the wraps should be similar to the size of the space left in the fabric. The thread should be tightly wrapped around the needle and flush with the fabric.

3 Hold the wrapped thread in place. Gently pull the needle and thread through the fabric. Continue pulling the thread so that the wrapped thread lays flat on the fabric, filling in the space.

4 Finish the bullion knot. Bring the needle back down through the fabric next to the end of the wrapped knot. This creates a single bullion knot.

CHAIN STITCH

The chain stitch creates a linked chain in a row on the front of the fabric.

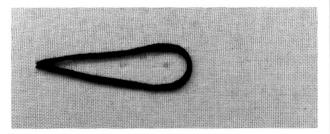

1 **Bring the needle up through the fabric from the back to begin the chain stitch row.** Bring the needle back down through the fabric at the starting point. Gently tug the thread to create an open loop on the front of the fabric in the direction of the chain link.

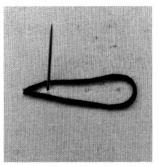 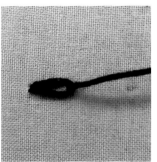

2 **Bring the needle up through the fabric inside the loop at the top point of the chain link.** Gently tug the thread so that the loop is flush with the fabric. This creates the first link in the chain.

3 **Continue adding links to the desired length.** Bring the needle back down through the fabric inside the previous loop. To finish the chain link row, bring the needle back down through the fabric on the outer edge of the chain link, creating a short, straight stitch to hold the link in place.

CORDED DETACHED BUTTONHOLE STITCH

This stitch looks like knitting and creates raised rows of stitches on the front of the fabric.

1 **Outline the shape with the back stitch.**

 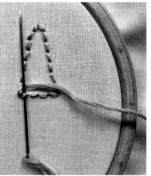

2 **Bring the needle up in the bottom-left corner of the shape.** Slide the needle under the first bottom back stitch and over the thread coming out of the fabric (the working thread).

3 **Gently tug so that the thread creates a connected loop on the front of the fabric.** Repeat along the entire row.

CORDED DETACHED BUTTONHOLE STITCH, continued

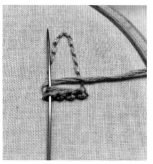

4 **With the first row stitched, slide the needle underneath the next row of outline back stitches.** Pull the thread to create a straight line above the row you just stitched. Slide the needle underneath the top stitch of the first row and this straight thread, then over the working thread.

5 **Gently tug the thread to create a connected loop in the second row on the front of the fabric.** Repeat along the entire row. Continue adding rows until the entire shape is filled in.

COUCHING STITCH

This versatile stitch is good for lines, outlines, or filling. Two threads are needed to stitch the horizontal and vertical parts.

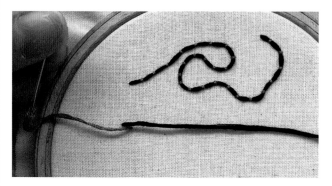

1 **Thread the needle with the thicker of the two threads.** Bring the needle up from the back of the fabric at the start of the line or section. Unthread the needle and lay this thread flat on the fabric in the direction of the line or section to be filled. Rethread and knot the needle with the thinner thread. Bring the thinner thread up from the back of the fabric about ⅛"–¼" (3.2–6.4mm) away from the start of the thicker thread.

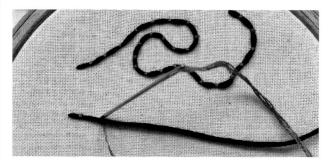

2 **Guide the thicker thread into place.** Then make a short stitch across the thicker thread to tack it into place. Repeat this by working along the thicker thread with spaced-out tacking stitches until you're almost at the end of the line or section. Tacking stitches can be spaced out with as many or as few as you'd prefer. I usually make a stitch every ¼" (6.4mm) along the thicker thread.

COUCHING STITCH, continued

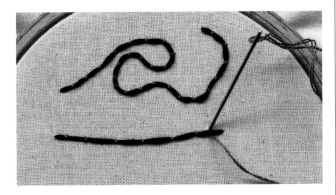

3 **To end the couching stitch, rethread the needle with the thicker thread.** Bring the needle back down through the fabric at the end of the line or section. Knot the thread. Rethread the needle with the thinner thread. Make the last tacking stitch along the thicker thread and knot the thread on the back of the fabric.

CRETAN STITCH

The Cretan stitch looks like *V*s connected along a center line.

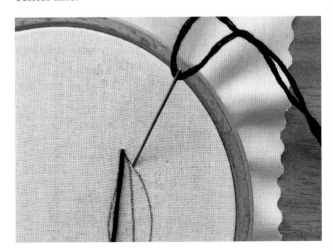

1 **Bring the needle up through the fabric at the tip of the leaf.** Hold the thread toward the center line of the leaf and bring the needle back through the fabric along the right outer edge of the leaf, creating an open *U* shape.

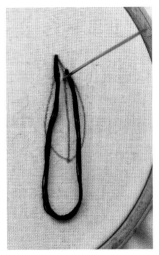 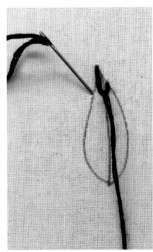

2 **Bring the needle up through the *U* along the center stem line.** Gently tug the thread taut so the *U* becomes a *V*. Hold the thread toward the center line and bring the needle down along the left outer edge of the leaf to begin the next *V*.

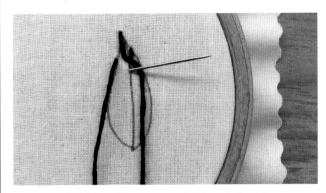

3 **Tug the thread to create a *U*, then bring the needle back up through the *U* along the center line.** Continue gently tugging the thread to create the *V*.

4 **Fill in the rest of the shape, alternating sides for each *V* stitch.** At the bottom of the shape, complete the last *V* stitch, then create a short straight stitch to secure the *V* at the base.

DETACHED CHAIN STITCH/LAZY DAISY

The detached chain stitch is also known as the lazy daisy. This stitch creates an individual link on the front of the fabric. By creating stitches from the same origin point and continuing in a circle, you can create a daisy.

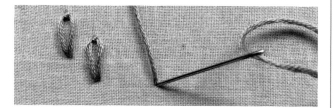

1 **Bring the needle up through the fabric from the back to the front.** Hold the thread in the direction of the detached chain and bring the needle back down through the fabric in the hole of the previous stitch.

2 **Gently tug the thread so that it forms an open loop on the front of the fabric.** Bring the needle up through the fabric, inside the loop, at the top point of the detached chain.

3 **Gently pull the thread so that it forms a link on the front of the fabric.** Bring the needle back through the fabric at the top outer edge of the loop to create a short straight stitch to hold the link in place. This creates one detached chain stitch.

FILLED DETACHED CHAIN STITCH

The filled detached chain stitch is a variation on the detached chain stitch that fills in the center space of the chain. This variation combines the detached chain stitch and the straight stitch—after the detached chain stitch is completed, you fill it in with the straight stitch.

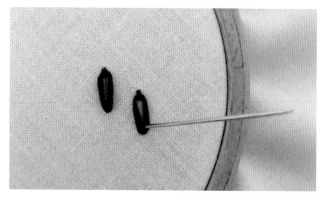

1 **Bring the needle up at the inside base of the detached chain stitch.**

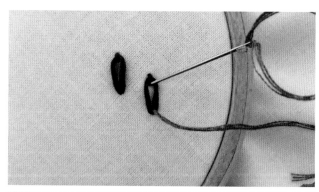

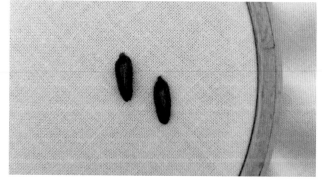

2 **Make a straight stitch that ends at the inside of the top of the detached chain stitch.**

FLY STITCH VARIATIONS

The fly stitch creates a V-shaped stitch. To make the basic fly stitch, I suggest following Steps 2–3 of the connected fly stitch.

This book uses three variations of the fly stitch: the connected fly stitch, double fly stitch, and reverse connected fly stitch. The connected fly stitch creates a line with *V*s spaced along it. The double fly stitch creates *V*s on top of one another. The reverse connected fly stitch is a way of working the stitch on top of the fabric.

Connected Fly Stitch

1 **Bring the needle up through the fabric at the top point of the connected fly stitch.** Make a short straight stitch forward along the line of the connected fly stitch.

2 **Bring the needle up through the fabric, slightly away from the left center of the straight stitch.** This will be the top-left point of the *V*. Bring the needle back down through the fabric on the opposite side of the straight stitch. This will be the top-right point of the *V*.

3 **Gently tug the thread so that this creates a loop of thread on the front of the fabric.** Now bring the needle back through the fabric at the bottom of the straight stitch.

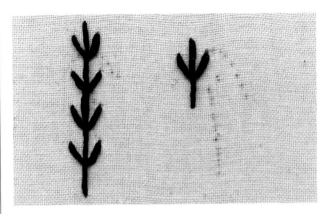

4 **Gently tug the thread so that the loop creates a *V* of thread that is flush with the fabric.**

5 **Repeat, adding straight stitches and *V*s until the line of connected fly stitches is complete.** To end the connected fly stitch, make a straight stitch of any desired length.

Double Fly Stitch

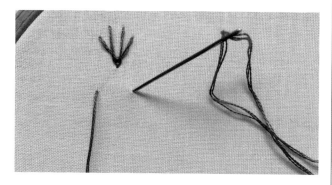

1 **Bring the needle up through the fabric at on one side of the V shape.** Then bring the needle back down through the fabric on the other side of the V.

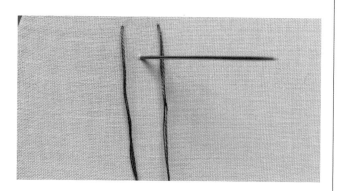

2 **Gently tug the thread so that it creates a *U* loop on the front of the fabric.** Bring the needle back of through the fabric inside the *U* where the bottom point of the V will be.

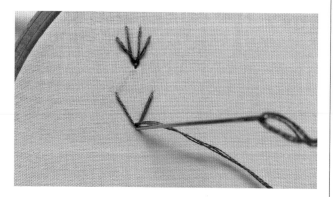

3 **Gently tug the thread so that the thread loop creates a *V* that is flush with the fabric.** Make a short stitch on the outer edge of the V to hold it in place.

4 **Create an inner *V* that is taller and thinner than the outer *V*.** Bring the needle up through the fabric at on one side of the *V* shape. Then bring the needle back down through the fabric to create the other side of the *V*.

5 **Gently tug the thread to create a *U* loop on the front of the fabric.** Bring the needle back through the fabric inside the *U* at the bottom point of the outer *V*.

6 **Gently tug the thread so that the thread loop creates a *V* that is flush with the fabric.** Make a short stitch on the outer edge of the V to hold it in place.

Reverse Connected Fly Stitch

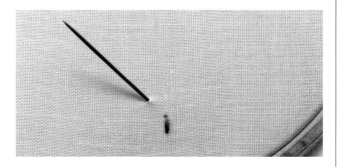

1 **Start at the bottom of the row of reverse fly stitches and make a short back stitch.** Bring the needle up through the fabric at the top corner of the first *V*.

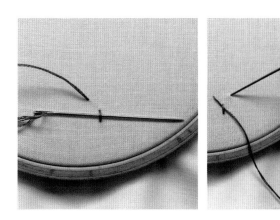

2 **Slide the needle underneath the back stitch.** Bring the needle back down through the fabric in the other top corner of the *V*.

3 Add the next back stitch between the reverse connected fly stitches.

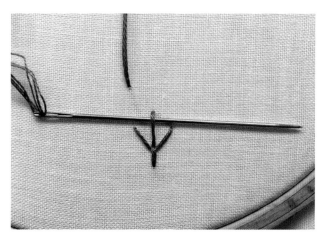

4 Repeat Step 2 to start the next fly stitch.

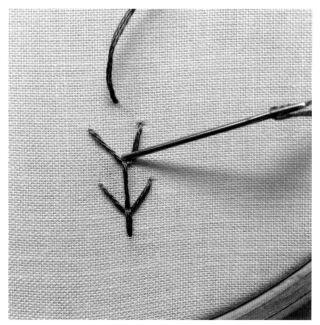

5 The reverse connected fly stitch ends with a back stitch.

FOUR-LEGGED KNOT

The four-legged knot looks like a plus sign with a knot in the center.

1 **Make a vertical stitch.** Then bring the needle up a short distance away from the center of the stitch.

2 **Lay the thread horizontally across the vertical stitch.** Bring the needle under the vertical stitch and over the horizontal thread.

3 **Gently tug so the wrapped thread is flush with the fabric.** Then bring the needle back down into the fabric to complete the horizontal line.

FRENCH KNOT

The French knot creates a round dot on the front of the fabric. This stitch is all about thread tension, so you might find it helpful to lay your hoop flat on the table, to work with both of your hands.

1 **Bring the needle up through the fabric at the center of the knot.** Pinch the thread in your nondominant hand about 3"–4" (7.6–10.2cm) from where the thread comes out of the front of the fabric.

TIP French knots are all about thread tension. If the thread is loose, the French knot will be loopy.

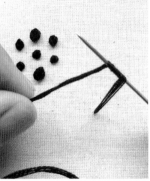

2 **Wrap the thread around the needle.** Keep it in between where the thread is pinched and where it is coming out of the fabric. The more times the thread is wrapped, the larger the knot will be.

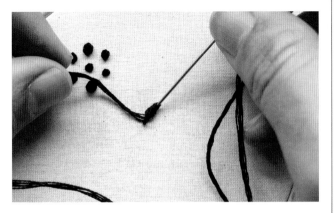

3 **Bring the needle back down through the fabric next to where the thread is coming up.**

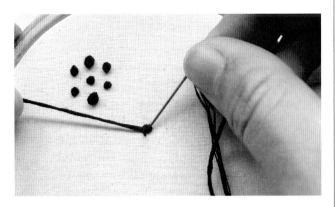

4 **Tighten the thread and finish the knot.** Before pushing the needle all the way through the fabric, gently tug the thread so that it is tightly wrapped around the needle and flush with the fabric. This creates one French knot.

GRANITOS STITCH

The granitos stitch creates a raised oval on the front of the fabric.

1 **Bring the needle up from the back of the fabric to the front.** Make a short stitch forward, the desired length of the granitos stitch.

2 **Bring the needle back up through the fabric at the start of the straight stitch.** Then go back down through the bottom of the straight stitch. Gently pull the thread close to the fabric, pressing it to the side of the straight stitch.

3 **Repeat on the other side, pressing the thread to the left of the stitch.** This creates one granitos stitch.

LADDER/INVISIBLE STITCH

The ladder or invisible stitch is used to join two pieces of fabric together seamlessly. This will be used to close the seams of the espadrille shoes (see page 121).

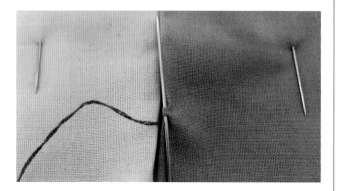

1 Bring the needle up from the inside of the fabric where the fabric will connect along the crease.

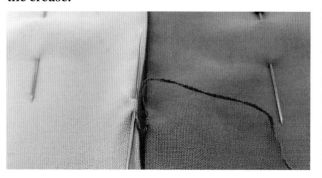

2 Directly across from where the thread is coming out of the fabric, bring the needle in and out of the other fabric along the crease. This stitch should be about ⅛" (3 2mm).

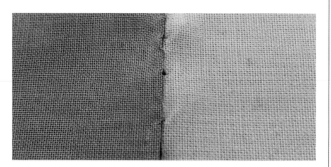

3 Gently tug the thread through the fabric. Repeat on the other side, then continue alternating sides with the stitches and gently tugging the thread so that the fabrics are stitched together and the thread is not visible.

LEAF STITCH

The leaf stitch name pretty much gives away what this stitch is great for stitching.

 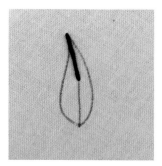

1 Bring the needle up through the back of the fabric at the top point of the leaf. Bring the needle back down through the fabric one stitch length away along the middle line of the leaf.

 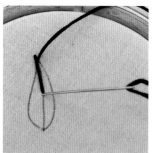

2 Bring the needle back up through the fabric along the outer edge of the leaf to the right of the first stitch. Then bring the needle back down slightly below the last stitch along the middle line.

3 Repeat on the opposite side by bringing the needle up from the back along the left outer edge of the leaf. Then bring the needle back down slightly below the last stitch along the middle line.

4 Repeat Steps 2 and 3 until the leaf is filled in.

LONG AND SHORT SATIN STITCH

The long and short satin stitch is great for filling in large areas as well as blending colors together.

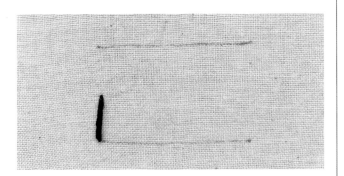

1 Bring the needle up through the fabric. Start at the bottom of the section that is to be filled. Make a straight stitch into the section.

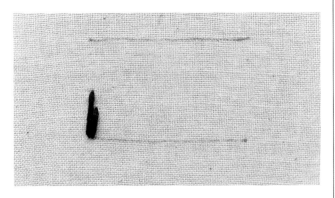

2 Bring the needle back up next to the start of the first stitch. Make a stitch that's either shorter or longer than the last stitch.

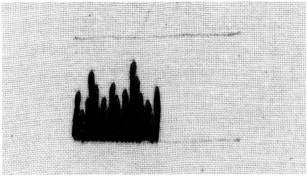

3 Continue filling in the shape with a horizontal row of stitches that vary in length.

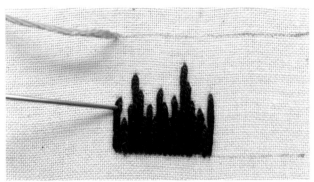

4 To add another row or blend another color, bring the needle up on the opposite side of the shape. Then make a straight stitch toward the end of the stitches that are filling the space. To connect the two stitches, bring the needle down into the stitch so that the ends slightly overlap.

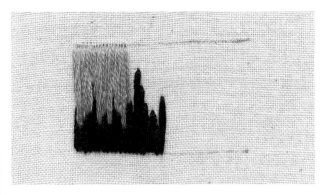

5 Bring the needle back up through the fabric next to the start of this stitch. Continue adding stitches in this row, blending the two rows together.

PADDED SATIN STITCH

The padded satin stitch is a satin stitch with padding underneath it. It's slightly more raised and fluffier than the satin stitch.

1 **To create the padded satin stitch, fill in the section with a filling stitch.** This can be the seed stitch, back stitch, or the satin stitch filled in using a different direction.

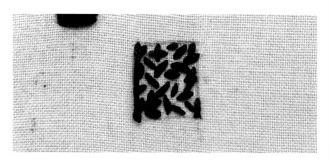

2 **Stitch the satin stitch over the filling stitches.** Bring the needle up from the back of the fabric at the bottom of the section. Create a straight stitch across to the other side of the section.

3 **Continue adding satin stitches.** Bring the needle up next to where the first stitch was started and then go across to the other side. Satin stitches should be close together, almost like they're hugging one another, and fill the section in the same direction.

RADIAL SATIN STITCH

The radial satin stitch creates a smooth fill that is stitched around a central point.

1 **Bring the needle up from the back to the front along the outer edge of the radial shape.** Make a straight satin stitch down toward the point of radiation.

2 **Bring the needle back up along the outer edge of the shape, next to the previous stitch.** Again, stitch toward the point of radiation, however, this stitch should be slightly shorter than the last one. Tuck the end of the stitch underneath the thread of the previous stitch.

3 **Repeat, making a shorter stitch next to the last.**

4 **Make a longer stitch next to these three stitches that goes from the outer edge to the point of radiation.** Then repeat the shorter and longer stitches as you stitch around the shape, until it is filled.

REVERSE CHAIN STITCH

The reverse chain stitch is similar to the chain stitch, creating a raised chain link on the front of the fabric. These stitches are interchangeable. While I prefer the reverse chain to the chain stitch, this version requires more space to create, so sometimes using one or the other is a better fit for the pattern and space that is being filled.

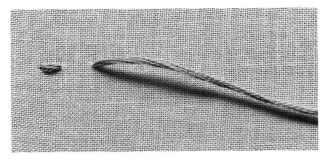

1 **The reverse chain stitch row is started with one short back stitch.** Similar to the back stitch, leave a space away from the previous stitch, then bring the needle up through the fabric.

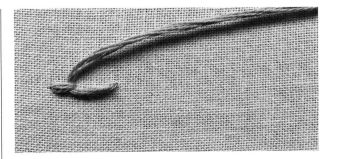

2 **Slide the needle underneath the back stitch.** Gently tug the thread so that it is flush with the fabric. Then bring the needle back down in the hole of the stitch, closing the chain link.

3 **Continue to add links to the chain by bringing the needle up a stitch's length away from the previous link.** Slide the needle under both strands of the link. Then close the loop by bringing the needle back down through the hole of the stitch.

TIP If the needle tip is getting caught in the stitches, flip the needle around and slide the eye under the thread. The eye is blunter and will help the needle from getting caught in the thread and splitting it apart.

RHODES STITCH

The Rhodes stitch is an overlapping stitch that creates a raised center.

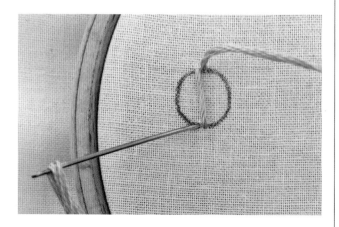

1 **Make a straight vertical stitch across the center of the shape.** Bring the needle up next to the start of the first stitch. Then stitch across the straight line, bringing the needle down on the other side of the stitch.

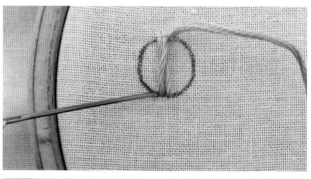

2 Continue stitching from one side of the shape to the other, overlapping the stitches until the shape is filled.

RIBBED SPIDERWEB STITCH

The ribbed spiderweb stitch is a woven stitch that creates a circle of raised lines on the front of the fabric.

1 **Make an uneven number of straight stitches starting at the outer edge of the circle and ending in the center point.**

2 **Bring the needle up near the center point beside one of the straight stitches.** Slide the needle underneath the two closest straight stitches.

3 Gently pull the thread underneath the straight stitches.

4 Slide the needle back underneath the second stitch you just went under and the stitch that follows. The working thread will wrap around the straight stitch.

5 Repeat Step 4 all the way around the circle until it is filled in. End the stitch by bringing the needle down through the fabric as you wrap around the last straight stitch.

SATIN STITCH

The satin stitch creates a solid fill of smooth color with all the stitches being made in the same direction.

1 Bring the needle up from the back of the fabric to the front at the bottom of the section. Create a straight stitch across to the other side of the section.

2 Continue adding satin stitches by bringing the needle up next to where the first stitch was started. Satin stitches should be close together, almost like they're hugging one another, and fill the section in the same direction. It's okay if they overlap.

SEED STITCH

The seed stitch creates short stitches in different directions. It looks like a scattering of seeds or confetti.

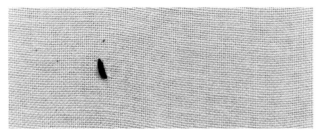

1 **Bring the needle up from the back of the fabric to the front.** Make a short stitch forward in any direction to fill the space.

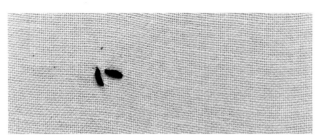

2 **Leave a space and bring the needle back up through the fabric.** Make another short stitch forward in a different direction.

3 **Continue filling the space with short, small stitches that go in different directions.**

TIP To add more texture, densely fill the section by overlapping the seed stitches.

SPLIT BACK STITCH

The split back stitch creates a line of stitches that connect into themselves.

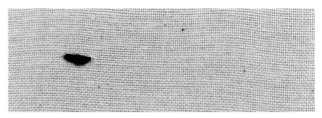

1 **Create one short back stitch along the row.** Bring the needle up from the back of the fabric to the front a stitch's length away from the starting point of the line and back down at the beginning of the line.

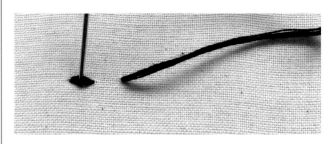

2 **Leave a space away from the previous stitch, along the line, and bring the needle back up through the fabric.** Bring the needle back down through the fabric in the middle of the last stitch, splitting the thread of the stitch.

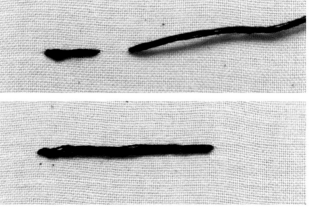

3 **Continue leaving a space and filling it in.** Bring the needle down in the middle of the last stitch until the line is complete.

STEM STITCH

The stem stitch creates a coiled rope on the front of the fabric.

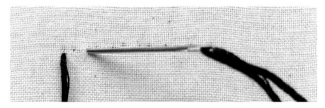

1 **Bring the needle up from the back of the fabric to the front at the start of the line.** Hold the thread off to one side of the line and bring the needle back down through the fabric a stitch's length away (about ⅛"–¼" [3.2-6.4mm]).

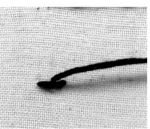

2 **Keep the loop of thread on the front of the fabric.** Bring the needle back up through the fabric in between where the thread is coming in and out of the fabric, along the same line. Then gently tug the thread loop so that it is flush with the fabric.

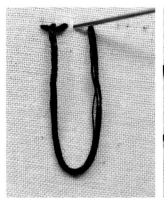

3 **Continue along the line.** Hold the thread off to the same side, bring the needle back down through the fabric a stitch's length away, then back up through the fabric in between where the thread is coming in and out of the fabric. To finish the stem line, bring the needle down through the fabric in the hole of the last stitch.

STRAIGHT STITCH

The straight stitch is a single straight line. It is sometimes referred to as a single satin stitch.

1 **Bring the needle up from the back of the fabric at the bottom point of the straight stitch.**

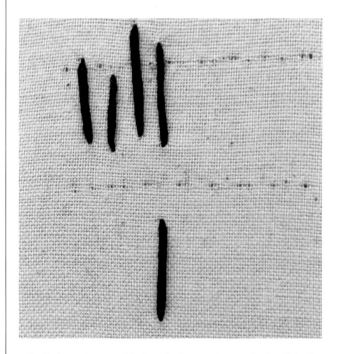

2 **Bring the needle back down through the fabric at the top point of the straight stitch.** This creates a single straight stitch.

WOVEN/WEAVE STITCH

The woven or weave stitch creates a grid pattern on the front of the fabric.

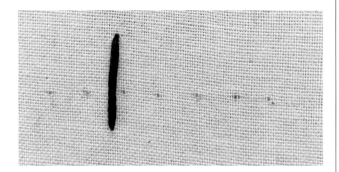

1 **Bring the needle up from the back of the fabric at the bottom corner of the section that will be filled.** Make a straight stitch across to the opposite side and gently tug the thread flush with the fabric.

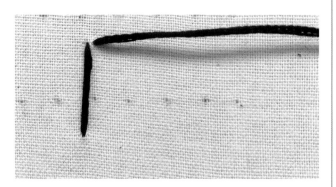

2 **Leave a small space on the same side where the needle went down through the fabric.** Bring the needle back up through the fabric. Then make a short stitch across to the other side of the shape.

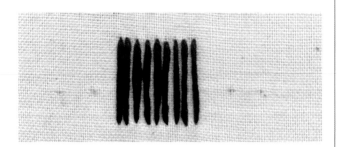

3 **Continue filling in the shape with straight parallel lines that are close to one another.**

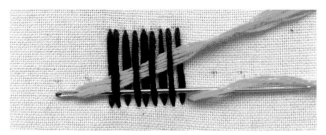

4 **Weave in the perpendicular rows.** Bring the threaded needle up through the fabric near the bottom corner of the section. Flip the needle around and weave the eye of the needle over, under, over, under the lines of thread, working the needle across to the opposite side.

5 **Gently tug the thread so that it is pulled through the rows and is flush with the fabric.** Then bring the needle down through the fabric to end the row. Bring the needle back up through the fabric slightly above the row that just ended.

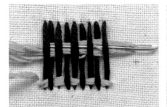 

6 **Weave the needle through the thread in an alternating pattern from the previous row.** Continue adding woven rows until the section is filled.

> **TIP** If the vertical and horizontal rows are spaced out, there will be spaces in the grid. For a tighter grid, stitch the rows closer together.

Projects

Are you ready to stitch something special onto your shoes? These projects include 15 different designs inspired by living in the Pacific Northwest, my travels, and things I love about nature. You'll swim with orcas, bead the clouds of a moonlit forest, buzz among bees in a wildflower garden, and more! The projects start with beginner-friendly designs and work up to more advanced stitching. As you work your way through these designs, you'll be able to try out new stitches and techniques, while creating your own unique footwear.

Colorful Clouds

Sunsets are some of my favorite views! I love how the colors in the sky change and the clouds seem to light up. This design plays with color and reimagines clouds at sunset.

What you'll need to create this design:

- Pattern (page 122)
- Canvas shoes
- Water-soluble transfer paper or carbon paper
- Pencil or transfer pen
- Scissors

- #5 embroidery needle or darning needle
- Needle grippers
- DMC embroidery thread colors: 19, 25, 349, 351, 352, 504, 550, 552, 554, 721, 754, 900, 3814, 3816, 3825, 3847, and Diamant D3821

COLOR AND STITCH GUIDE

This diagram shows what colors and stitches are used within the design. For detailed instructions on how to create each stitch, see the Stitch Glossary starting on page 22.

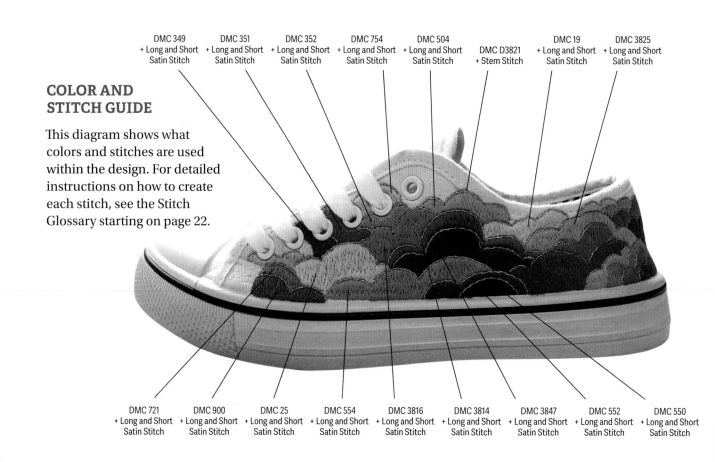

DMC 349 + Long and Short Satin Stitch

DMC 351 + Long and Short Satin Stitch

DMC 352 + Long and Short Satin Stitch

DMC 754 + Long and Short Satin Stitch

DMC 504 + Long and Short Satin Stitch

DMC D3821 + Stem Stitch

DMC 19 + Long and Short Satin Stitch

DMC 3825 + Long and Short Satin Stitch

DMC 721 + Long and Short Satin Stitch

DMC 900 + Long and Short Satin Stitch

DMC 25 + Long and Short Satin Stitch

DMC 554 + Long and Short Satin Stitch

DMC 3816 + Long and Short Satin Stitch

DMC 3814 + Long and Short Satin Stitch

DMC 3847 + Long and Short Satin Stitch

DMC 552 + Long and Short Satin Stitch

DMC 550 + Long and Short Satin Stitch

1 **Fill in the darkest teal clouds.** 3 strands of DMC 3847 + Long and Short Satin Stitch. Use vertical stitches. For Steps 1–7, if parts of the clouds are shorter than ¼" (6.4mm), use the Satin Stitch instead.

2 **Fill in the second layer of teal clouds.** 3 strands of DMC 3814 + Long and Short Satin Stitch.

3 **Fill in the third layer of teal clouds.** 3 strands of DMC 3816 + Long and Short Satin Stitch.

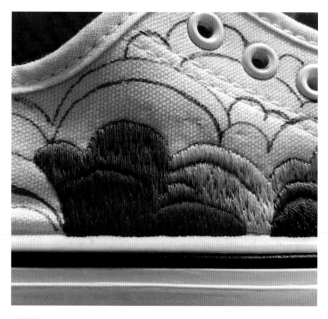

4 **Fill in the final layer of teal clouds.** 3 strands of DMC 504 + Long and Short Satin Stitch.

5 **Repeat Steps 1 through 4 to fill in the orange cloud layers.** 3 strands of DMC 900, 3 strands of DMC 721, 3 strands of DMC 3825, and 3 strands of DMC 19 + Long and Short Satin Stitch.

6 Repeat Steps 1 through 4 to fill in the purple cloud layers. 3 strands of DMC 550, 3 strands of DMC 552, 3 strands of DMC 554, and 3 strands of DMC 25 + Long and Short Satin Stitch.

7 Repeat Steps 1 through 4 to fill in the coral cloud layers. 3 strands of DMC 349, 3 strands of DMC 351, 3 strands of DMC 352, and 3 strands of DMC 754 + Long and Short Satin Stitch.

8 Outline the cloud layers. DMC Gold Diamant D3821 + Stem Stitch. Make small stitches, holding the thread toward the outer edge of the curve. This will help the outline hug the curves better and cover up any unevenness between the cloud layers.

Tips for working with metallic thread:

Metallic thread tends to unravel, can be a bit difficult to pull through the fabric, and is a bit more likely to break. The following tips will help.

- Cut a shorter length than usual. I work with 12"–18" (30.5–45.7cm) lengths.
- Use thread gloss to keep the thread from unraveling and make it easier to pull through the fabric.
- Be gentle when stitching. Do not tug too hard, or it will break.

Orcas

I live in the Pacific Northwest. Orcas can be seen swimming off the coast. When I take my dogs for a walk, we love to stroll up to the crest of a hill that overlooks Vashon Island. Orcas can often be seen swimming by throughout the spring and summer. Have fun stitching your own orca sighting!

What you'll need to create this design:

- Patterns (page 122)
- Canvas shoes
- Water-soluble transfer paper or carbon paper
- Pencil or transfer pen
- Scissors
- #5 embroidery needle or darning needle
- Needle grippers
- DMC embroidery thread colors: Blanc, C310 (Mouline Etoile), 3756, 3761, and 3810

COLOR AND STITCH GUIDE

This diagram shows what colors and stitches are used within the design. For detailed instructions on how to create each stitch, see the Stitch Glossary starting on page 22.

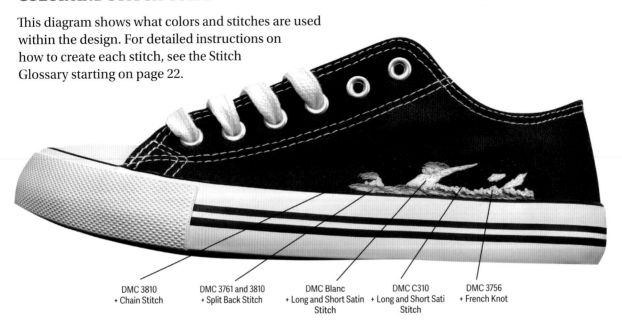

DMC 3810
+ Chain Stitch

DMC 3761 and 3810
+ Split Back Stitch

DMC Blanc
+ Long and Short Satin Stitch

DMC C310
+ Long and Short Sati Stitch

DMC 3756
+ French Knot

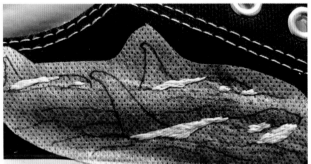

1 **Fill in the white sections of the orcas.** 3 strands of DMC Blanc + Long and Short Satin Stitch. These stitches should run the length of the shapes filled.

2 **Fill in the black sections of the orcas.** 3 strands of DMC C310 + Long and Short Satin Stitch.

TIP Etoile thread is bouncier than standard cotton thread. Be gentle with it so it doesn't tear when you pull it through the fabric. This thread can also be fuzzier than cotton thread. Use your needle to comb it down toward the fabric.

3 **Add the wave tops.** 3 strands of DMC 3810 + Chain Stitch. Fill in the top portion of each wave. This will be the darker parts of the water.

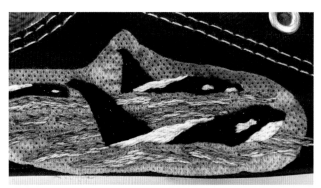

4 **Fill in the waves.** 2 strands of DMC 3761 and 1 strand of DMC 3810 + Split Back Stitch. Fill in the variegated sections of the water. Fill 2–3 rows below the top wave or until the section reaches the sole of the shoe. These lines should follow the curves of the wave tops.

5 **Add the foam.** 3 strands of DMC 3756 + French Knot.

Moonlit Forest

As a girl, I went on a lot of camping trips with the Girl
Scouts. We sometimes went on night hikes that terrified me.
This design reimagines the forest at night to be whimsical,
with a glowing moon and beaded clouds.

What you'll need to create this design:

- Patterns (page 123)
- High-top canvas shoes
- Water-soluble transfer paper or carbon paper
- Transfer pen or pencil
- Scissors
- #5 embroidery needle
- Needle grippers
- DMC embroidery thread colors: 02, 03, 310, 414, 453, and 3866
- 8/0 and 6/0 seed beads in blues and purples

COLOR AND STITCH GUIDE

This diagram shows what colors and stitches are used within the design. For detailed
instructions on how to create each stitch, see the Stitch Glossary starting on page 22.

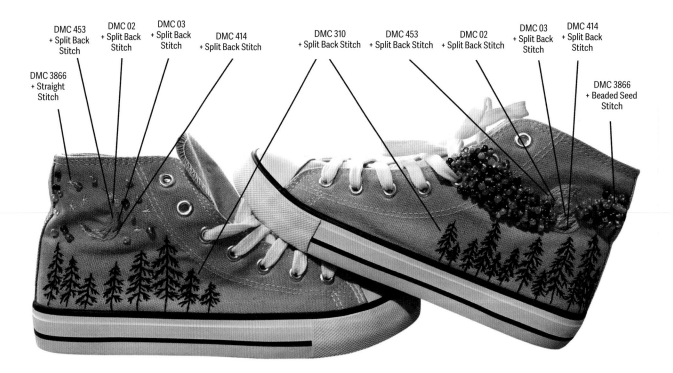

DMC 453 + Split Back Stitch

DMC 02 + Split Back Stitch

DMC 03 + Split Back Stitch

DMC 414 + Split Back Stitch

DMC 310 + Split Back Stitch

DMC 453 + Split Back Stitch

DMC 02 + Split Back Stitch

DMC 03 + Split Back Stitch

DMC 414 + Split Back Stitch

DMC 3866 + Straight Stitch

DMC 3866 + Beaded Seed Stitch

FULL MOON INSTRUCTIONS

1 Add the trees. 2 strands of DMC 310 + Split Back Stitch. Start with the trunk and then add the branches. As the stitching gets closer to the heal, you may need to wiggle the needle gently to push it through the layers of fabric. Needle grippers will also help pull the needle through the fabric.

2 **Fill in the darkest parts of the moon.** 3 strands of DMC 414 + Split Back Stitch.

3 **Fill in the second-darkest moon color.** 3 strands of DMC 03 + Split Back Stitch.

4 **Fill in the third-darkest moon color.** 3 strands of DMC 02 + Split Back Stitch.

5 **Fill in the final moon color.** 3 strands of DMC 453 + Split Back Stitch. Follow the curve of the moon and leave space to stitch the clouds.

6 **Fill in the clouds.** 3 strands of DMC 3866 + Beaded Seed Stitch. I used an assortment of purple and blue seed beads. To get a solid fill, add beads near each other, then go back and fill in any gaps between beads. The beads that fill the gaps will sit slightly higher and add more texture to the clouds.

CRESCENT MOON INSTRUCTIONS

  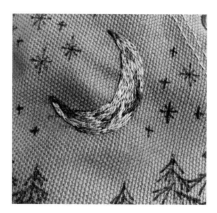

1 **Fill in the crescent moon as you filled in the full moon, working from darkest to lightest.** 3 strands of DMC 414, DMC 03, DMC 02, and DMC 453 + Split Back Stitch.

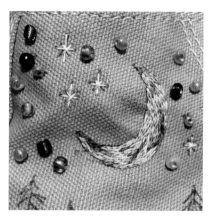

3 **Add the smaller stars.** 3 strands of DMC 3866 + Beaded Seed Stitch. The smaller stars are single seed beads. After adding a beaded star, knot the thread and move to the next closest star. The knot on the back adds extra protection to the stitching and ensures that if one bead detaches, they won't all detach.

2 **Add the eight-pointed stars.** 2 strands of DMC 3866 + Straight Stitch. Create the vertical and horizontal stitches, then add the diagonal points.

4 **Add the trees.** 2 strands of DMC 310 + Split Back Stitch. Follow Step 1 of the Full Moon Instructions.

Slither By

I will be the first to admit it—snakes freak me out! But a while back, a friend who makes gorgeous ceramic snakes challenged me to face my fear of snakes and embroider one. While I'm still not a snake fan, I did enjoy embroidering this squiggly snake body and adding beads as embellishments. I hope you do, too.

What you'll need to create this design:

- Pattern (page 123)
- Low-rise canvas shoes
- Water-soluble transfer paper or carbon paper
- Transfer pen or pencil

- Scissors
- Darning needle
- Beading needle
- Needle grippers

- DMC embroidery thread colors: ECRU, 16, 310, 349, 890, 905, and 3847
- 10/0 red seed beads
- 3–6mm white bugle beads

COLOR AND STITCH GUIDE

This diagram shows what colors and stitches are used within the design. For detailed instructions on how to create each stitch, see the Stitch Glossary starting on page 22.

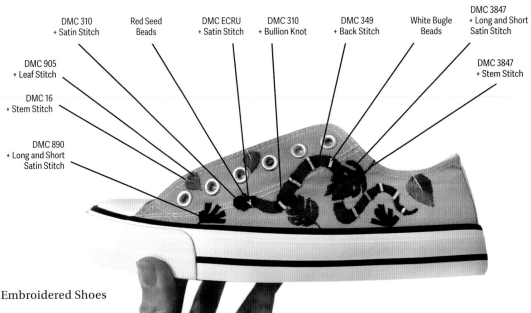

DMC 310 + Satin Stitch

Red Seed Beads

DMC ECRU + Satin Stitch

DMC 310 + Bullion Knot

DMC 349 + Back Stitch

White Bugle Beads

DMC 3847 + Long and Short Satin Stitch

DMC 905 + Leaf Stitch

DMC 16 + Stem Stitch

DMC 890 + Long and Short Satin Stitch

DMC 3847 + Stem Stitch

INSTRUCTIONS

1 **Fill in the philodendron leaves.** 3 strands of DMC 905 + Leaf Stitch.

2 **Add the philodendron stems.** 2 strands of DMC 16 + Stem Stitch. Start in the center line of the philodendron leaves and work toward the bottom of the stem line.

3 **Fill in the fan palm leaves.** 3 strands of DMC 890 + Long and Short Satin Stitch. These stitches should be made lengthwise.

4 **Fill in the monstera leaves.** 3 strands of DMC 3847 + Long and Short Satin Stitch. These stitches should be made diagonally from the outer edge toward the center line.

5 **Add the monstera stems.** 3 strands of DMC 3847 + Stem Stitch.

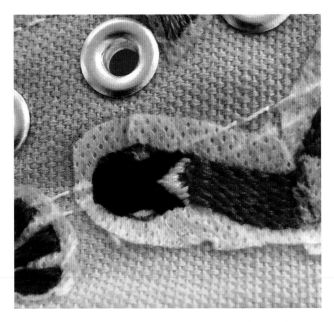

6 **Fill in the red stripes on the snake's body.** 3 strands of DMC 349 + Back Stitch. These back stitches should be made in rows along the length of the body, following the curves.

7 **Fill in the black section of the snake's head.** 2 strands of DMC 310 + Satin Stitch. These stitches should be made diagonally toward the center line.

8 **Fill in the cream section of the snake's head.** 3 strands of DMC ECRU + Satin Stitch.

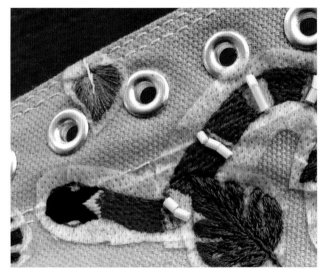
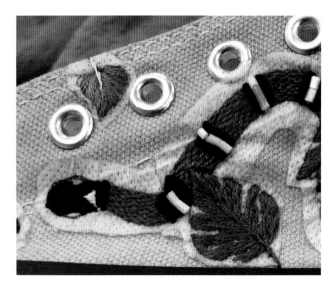

9 Add the white bugle bead stripes. 1 strand of DMC ECRU + Beaded Back Stitch. Add a line of bugle beads to the center of each stripe on the snake. Make the stitches from one side of the snake to the other. For these stitches, you may need to switch to a beading needle with a thinner eye.

10 Fill in the black stripes on the snake's body. 3 strands of DMC 310 + Bullion Knot. Add these stripes on either side of the bugle beads and at the base of the snake's head.

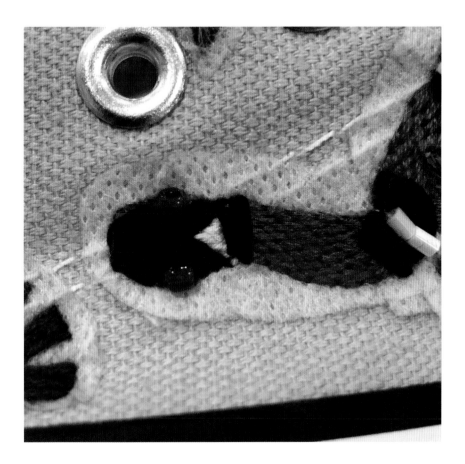

11 Add the snake's eyes. 2 strands of DMC 349 + Beaded Back Stitch. If you use a different color of seed bead for the eyes, match the thread color to the bead color.

Mountain Sunset

These gray mountain ranges were inspired by road trips over the Snoqualmie Pass. Before I moved to the Seattle area, my now husband and I dated long distance. Thankfully that distance was only a three-hour drive, and we saw each other every few weekends. For this design you'll play with blending colors to create a vibrant sunset behind mountain ranges.

What you'll need to create this design:

- Patterns (page 124)
- Canvas shoes
- Water-soluble transfer paper or carbon paper

- Pencil or transfer pen
- Scissors
- Darning needle
- Needle grippers

- DMC embroidery thread colors: 26, 159, 168, 415, C823, 3042, 3747, 4190, 4200, and 4210

COLOR AND STITCH GUIDE

This diagram shows what colors and stitches are used within the design. For detailed instructions on how to create each stitch, see the Stitch Glossary starting on page 22.

DMC 4200
+ Long and Short Satin Stitch

DMC 4210
+ Long and Short Satin Stitch

DMC 159 and C823
+ Weave Stitch

DMC C823
+ Reverse Chain Stitch

DMC 159
+ Long and Short Satin Stitch

DMC 4190
+ Long and Short Satin Stitch

DMC 415 and 159
+ Chain Stitch

DMC 26 and 3042
+ Chain Stitch

DMC 3747
+ Long and Short Satin Stitch

DMC 168
+ Chain Stitch

INSTRUCTIONS

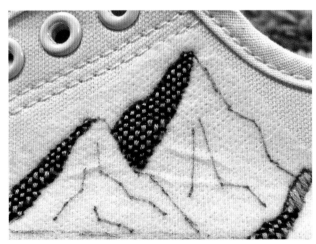

1 **Fill in the back sides of the mountains on the left shoe.** 3 strands of DMC 159 and 3 strands of DMC C823 + Woven/Weave Stitch. Use the 3 strands of DMC 159 to create the vertical rows of the weave stitch. The rows should be about a thread width apart so that the shoe color won't show through once the second color is woven in. Use the 3 strands of DMC C823 to fill in the horizontal rows of the weave stitch.

2 **Outline the mountain edges and details.** 3 strands of DMC C823 + Revere Chain Stitch.

3 **Fill in the first mountain.** 3 strands of DMC 159 + Long and Short Satin Stitch. These stitches should be made vertically in rows from the bottom of the mountain to the top.

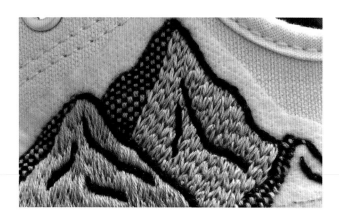

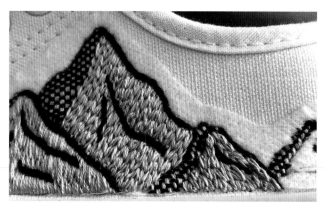

4 **Fill in the second mountain.** 2 strands of DMC 415 and 1 strand of DMC 159 + Chain Stitch. These stitches should align with the edge of the woven section on the left to fill in the mountain at an angle.

5 **Fill in the third mountain.** 2 strands of DMC 26 and 2 strands of DMC 3042 + Chain Stitch. These stitches should align with the mountain's outline on the right to fill in the mountain at an angle that is perpendicular to the stitched rows of the second mountain.

6 **Fill in the fourth mountain.** 3 strands of DMC 3747 + Long and Short Satin Stitch. Start with a row at the bottom of the mountain and fill in the rows toward the top.

7 **Fill in the fifth mountain.** 3 strands of DMC 168 + Chain Stitch. Use the mountain's outline on the right as a guide to create the first angled row of stitches.

8 **Add the first five mountains to the right shoe, matching the colors and stitches from Steps 1 through 7.**

9 **Add the sixth mountain to the right shoe.** 2 strands of DMC 26 and 2 strands of 3042 + Chain Stitch. Fill in this mountain following the angle of the mountain's outline on the right.

10 **Fill in the first section of the sky.** 3 strands of DMC 4210 + Long and Short Satin Stitch. Fill in the portion of the sky closest to the shortest mountains with horizontal stitches.

11 **Fill in the next section of the sky.** 3 strands of DMC 4200 + Long and Short Satin Stitch.

12 **Fill in the last section of the sky.** 3 strands of DMC 4190 + Long and Short Satin Stitch.

Spring Bird

These shoes celebrate spring. I love waking up on a spring morning to hear birds chirping outside my window and see which of the plants have started to bloom. With this design, you'll stitch spring birds surrounded by flowers blossoming on tree branches.

What you'll need to create this design:

- Pattern (page 125)
- Low-rise canvas shoes
- Water-soluble transfer paper or carbon paper

- Transfer pen or pencil
- Scissors
- Darning needle
- Needle grippers

- DMC embroidery thread colors: 08, 10, 23, 224, 433, 471, 472, 898, 928, 930, 932, and 3866

COLOR AND STITCH GUIDE

This diagram shows what colors and stitches are used within the design. For detailed instructions on how to create each stitch, see the Stitch Glossary starting on page 22.

DMC 928
+ Long and Short Satin Stitch

DMC 930
+ Long and Short Satin Stitch

DMC 932
+ Long and Short Satin Stitch

DMC 08
+ Straight Stitch

DMC 898
+ Straight Stitch

DMC 433
+ Reverse Chain Stitch

DMC 08
+ Satin Stitch

DMC 3866
+ Long and Short Satin Stitch

DMC 224
+ Detached Chain Stitch

DMC 224
+ Granitos Stitch

DMC 471 and 472
+ Leaf Stitch

DMC 23
+ Straight Stitch

DMC 10
+ French Knot

1 **Fill in the tree branch.** 3 strands of DMC 433 + Reverse Chain Stitch. Start with the central section, then add in the smaller branches. As the branches taper off, overlap the rows of stitches to blend them together.

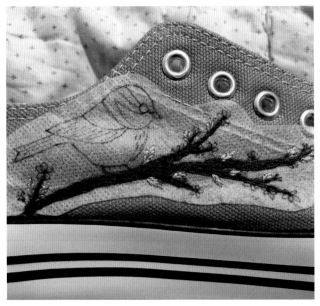

2 **Add texture and branch details.** 2 strands of DMC 898 + Straight Stitch.

3 **Add the small leaves.** 2 strands of DMC 472 and 1 strand of DMC 471 + Leaf Stitch.

4 **Add the flower buds.** 3 strands of DMC 224 + Granitos Stitch.

5 **Add the flower blossoms.** 3 strands of DMC 224 + Detached Chain Stitch.

6 **Fill in the flower petals.** 2 strands of DMC 23 + Straight Stitch. Fill in the centers of the detached chain stitches.

7 **Add the centers to the flowers.** 2 strands of DMC 10 + French Knot.

8 **Add the dark blue sections of the bird.** 3 strands of DMC 930 + Long and Short Satin Stitch. The stitches along the wing are made diagonally from left to right. The stitches along the head follow the length of the shape.

9 **Fill in the medium blue sections of the bird.** 3 strands of DMC 932 + Long and Short Satin Stitch. Fill in each section lengthwise.

10 **Fill in the lightest blue sections of the bird.** 3 strands of DMC 928 + Long and Short Satin Stitch. The stitches along the wing are made diagonally from left to right. The stitches along the head follow the length of the shape.

11 **Fill in the bird's chest and head.** 3 strands of DMC 3866 + Long and Short Satin Stitch. Fill in each section lengthwise, following the curve of the shape.

12 **Fill in the bird's eye and beak.** 2 strands of DMC 08 + Satin Stitch.

13 **Add the bird's legs and feet.** 2 strands of DMC 08 + Straight Stitch. Make a single straight stitch for the leg, then add three prongs for the feet.

14 **Add accents to the bird's chest.** 2 strands of DMC 08 + Seed Stitch. Scatter a few seed stitches on the bird's chest.

Strawberry Delight

When I was growing up, we had strawberries and raspberries growing in our backyard. During the summer, we'd pick fresh fruit and eat it straight from the plant. While it was sometimes prickly to find the berries, it was always worth it. This design captures the sweetness of strawberries.

Here's what you'll need to create this design:

- Pattern (page 125)
- Low-rise canvas shoes
- Water-soluble transfer paper or carbon paper

- Transfer pen or pencil
- Scissors
- Darning needle
- Needle grippers

- DMC embroidery thread colors: 746, 3051, 3348, 3712, 3774, and 3831

COLOR AND STITCH GUIDE

This diagram shows what colors and stitches are used within the design. For detailed instructions on how to create each stitch, see the Stitch Glossary starting on page 22.

DMC 3712 and 3831 + Cordered Detached Buttonhole Stitch

DMC 3051 and 3348 + Granitos Stitch

DMC 746 + Seed Stitch

DMC 3774 + Granitos Stitch

DMC 3051 + Stem Stitch

DMC 3051 + Detached Chain Stitch

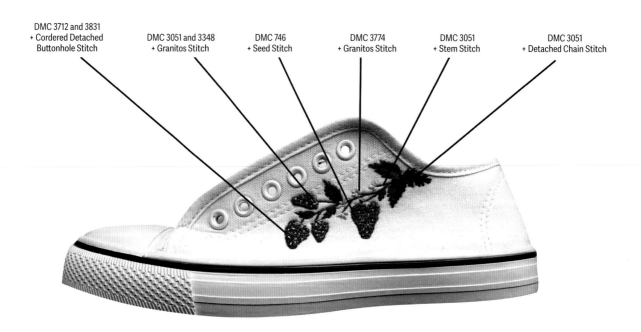

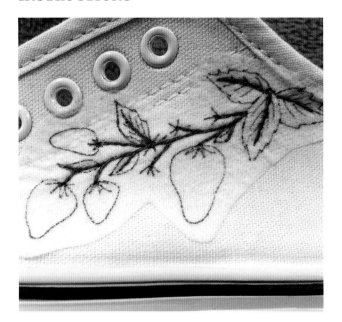

1 **Add the stems and center leaf lines.** 2 strands of DMC 3051 + Stem Stitch.

2 **Fill in the leaves.** 2 strands of DMC 3051 + Detached Chain Stitch. The detached chain stitches should start at the outer edge of the leaf and end at the center line.

3 **Fill in the strawberries.** 2 strands of DMC 3712 and 2 strands of DMC 3831 + Corded Detached Buttonhole Stitch.

4 **Add the tops to the strawberries.** 2 strands of DMC 3348 and 1 strand of DMC 3051 + Granitos Stitch.

5 **Add the flowers.** 3 strands of DMC 3774 + Granitos Stitch.

6 **Add the seeds.** 2 strands of DMC 746 + Seed Stitch.

Spiderwebs and Plants

Since becoming a homeowner, I have found that my grand ideas of gardening have flown out the window. I thought it would be fun to plan out my yard and plant greenery. What I didn't realize is all the upkeep that needs to happen to maintain such a plan! My greenery is now forlorn and cobwebby. This design is a playful rendition of the current state of my yard.

What you will need to create this design:

- Pattern (page 124)
- High-top canvas shoes
- Water-soluble transfer paper
- Pencil or transfer pen

- Scissors
- #5 embroidery needle
- Needle grippers

- DMC embroidery thread colors: 367, 368, 472, 500, 503, 731, 733, 801, and 4150

COLOR AND STITCH GUIDE

This diagram shows what colors and stitches are used within the design. For detailed instructions on how to create each stitch, see the Stitch Glossary starting on page 22.

DMC 500
+ Split Back Stitch

DMC 503
+ Double Fly Stitch

DMC 4150
+ Back Stitch

DMC 472 and 733
+ Couching Stitch

DMC 472
+ Leaf Stitch

DMC 368
+ Split Back Stitch

DMC 367 and 368
+ Cretan Stitch

DMC 731
+ Filled Detached Chain Stitch

DMC 801
+ Split Back Stitch

INSTRUCTIONS

1 **Add the first plant's stems.** 3 strands of DMC 500 + Split Back Stitch.

2 **Add the leaves.** 3 strands of DMC 503 + Double Fly Stitch.

3 **Add the second plant's stems.** 6 strands of DMC 733 and 2 strands of DMC 472 + Couching Stitch. Use DMC 733 as the laid threads and DMC 472 as the tacking threads.

4 **Add the leaves.** 4 strands of DMC 472 + Leaf Stitch.

5 **Add the third plant's stem.** 3 strands of DMC 368 + Split Back Stitch.

6 **Add the leaves.** 2 strands of DMC 367 and 1 strand of DMC 368 + Cretan Stitch.

7 **Add the fourth plant's stem.** 2 strands of DMC 801 + Split Back Stitch.

8 **Add the leaves.** 3 strands of DMC 731 + Filled Detached Chain Stitch.

9 **Add the spiderwebs.** 1 strand of DMC 4150 + Back Stitch. Start with the lines that meet at the center point, then work in circles from the center toward the outer edge.

Southwest Dream

I love the desert! I recently had the opportunity to hike the
Valley of Fire State Park and Zion National Park. I loved that the rock
formations were vibrant pinks and oranges. This design plays
with those colors to create a soft, dreamy desert.

What you'll need to create this design:

- Pattern (page 125)
- High-top canvas shoes
- Water-soluble transfer paper or carbon paper
- Pencil or transfer pen
- Scissors
- Darning needle
- Needle grippers
- DMC embroidery thread colors: 21, 223, 224, 355, 522, 524, 731, 758, 3721, and 3830

COLOR AND STITCH GUIDE

This diagram shows what colors and stitches are used within the design. For detailed
instructions on how to create each stitch, see the Stitch Glossary starting on page 22.

DMC 223
+ Long and Short
Satin Stitch

DMC 224
+ Back Stitch

DMC 522
and 524
+ Straight Stitch

DMC 223
and 3721
+ Couching Stitch

DMC 355
+ Long and Short
Satin Stitch

DMC 3830
+ Long and Short
Satin Stitch

DMC 731
+ Split Back
Stitch

DMC 21 and 758
+ Weave Stitch

DMC 21
+ Long and Short Satin
Stitch

DMC 731
+ Reverse Chain
Stitch

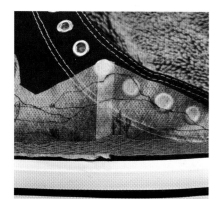

1 **Fill in the bottom landscape layer.** 2 strands of DMC 21 + Long and Short Satin Stitch. These stitches should be made horizontally across the landscape layer.

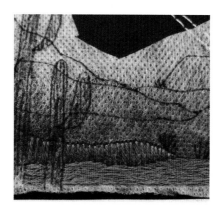

2 **Fill in the second landscape layer.** 2 strands of DMC 21 and 2 strands of DMC 758 + Woven/Weave Stitch. Use the 2 strands of DMC 21 to create the vertical rows of the weave stitch. Use the 2 strands of DMC 758 to fill in the horizontal rows of the weave stitch.

TIP If needed, flip the needle around and use the eye to weave through the thread. The eye is blunter, so it's easier to weave with.

3 **Fill in the third landscape layer.** 2 strands of DMC 3830 + Long and Short Satin Stitch. Make these stitches horizontally. Stitch around the larger cacti to leave space, but stitch over where the smaller cacti and plants will overlap this layer. We'll add those in later.

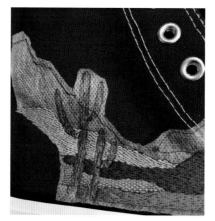

4 **Fill in the fourth landscape layer.** 2 strands of DMC 224 + Back Stitch. Make these stitches in diagonal rows. Each row should be offset from the previous, like a brick wall.

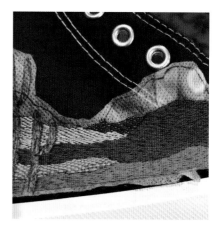

5 **Fill in the fifth landscape layer.** 3 strands of DMC 3721 and 2 strands of DMC 223 + Couching Stitch. Use DMC 3721 as the laid threads and DMC 223 as the tacking threads. Start at the bottom of the space and work horizontally across the section in rows until the space is filled.

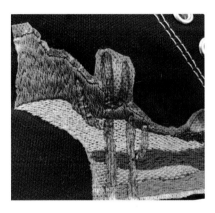

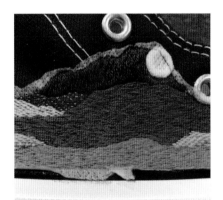

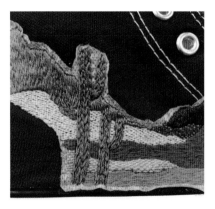

6 **Fill in the top-left landscape layer.** 2 strands of DMC 223 + Long and Short Satin Stitch. Make these stitches vertically.

7 **Fill in the top-right landscape layer.** 2 strands of DMC 355 + Long and Short Satin Stitch. Make these stitches vertically.

8 **Add the large cacti.** 3 strands of DMC 731 + Reverse Chain Stitch. Make these stitches in vertical rows. Start with the centers, then add the cactus arms.

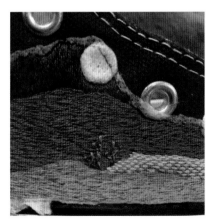

9 **Add the small cacti.** 2 strands of DMC 731 + Split Back Stitch.

10 **Add the light sagebrush.** 1 strand of DMC 522 + Straight Stitch. These stitches should vary in length and radiate from a central point.

11 **Add the dark sagebrush.** Use 1 strand of DMC 524 + Straight Stitch.

Pond Life

My parents' house has an irrigation pond behind it.
Growing up, my middle sister and I would try to play by
it and the marshy cattails nearby, even though this was
strictly forbidden by our mom. This design imagines
what plant and animal life we might have seen.

COLOR AND STITCH GUIDE

This diagram shows what colors and stitches are used within the design. For detailed
instructions on how to create each stitch, see the Stitch Glossary starting on page 22.

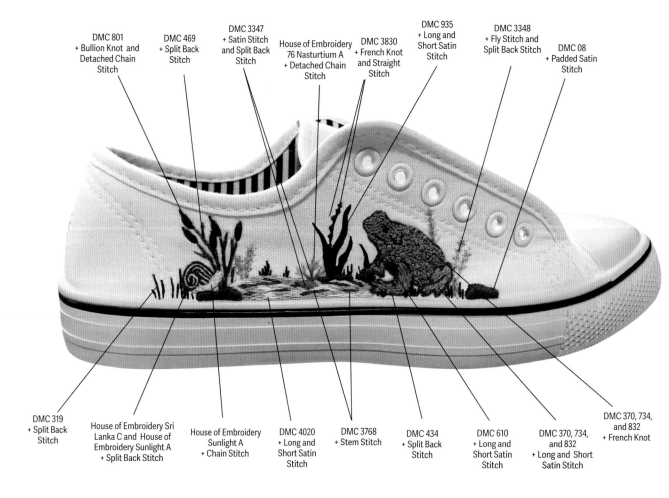

DMC 801
+ Bullion Knot and
Detached Chain
Stitch

DMC 469
+ Split Back
Stitch

DMC 3347
+ Satin Stitch
and Split Back
Stitch

House of Embroidery
76 Nasturtium A
+ Detached Chain
Stitch

DMC 3830
+ French Knot
and Straight
Stitch

DMC 935
+ Long and
Short Satin
Stitch

DMC 3348
+ Fly Stitch and
Split Back Stitch

DMC 08
+ Padded Satin
Stitch

DMC 319
+ Split Back
Stitch

House of Embroidery Sri
Lanka C and House of
Embroidery Sunlight A
+ Split Back Stitch

House of Embroidery
Sunlight A
+ Chain Stitch

DMC 4020
+ Long and
Short Satin
Stitch

DMC 3768
+ Stem Stitch

DMC 434
+ Split Back
Stitch

DMC 610
+ Long and
Short Satin
Stitch

DMC 370, 734,
and 832
+ Long and Short
Satin Stitch

DMC 370, 734,
and 832
+ French Knot

What you'll need to create this design:

- Pattern (page 125)
- Canvas shoes
- Water-soluble transfer paper or carbon paper
- Pencil or transfer pen
- Scissors

- #5 embroidery needle or darning needle
- Needle grippers
- DMC embroidery thread colors: 08, 319, 370, 434, 469, 610, 734, 801, 832, 935, 3347, 3348, 3768, 3830, and 4020
- House of Embroidery thread colors: 76 Nasturtium A, Sri Lanka C, and Sunlight A

1 Add the dark water ripples to the pond. 4 strands of DMC 3768 + Stem Stitch.

2 Fill in the pond. 3 strands of DMC 4020 + Long and Short Satin Stitch. Make these stitches horizontally across the length of the pond.

3 Fill in the rocks. 6 strands of DMC 08 + Padded Satin Stitch.

4 Add the V-shaped plants. 2 strands of DMC 3348 + Connected Fly Stitch and Split Back Stitch. Use the connected fly stitch to create the *V*s, then extend the stems of the plants with the split back stitch.

5 Add the tops of the cattails. 3 strands of DMC 801 + Bullion Knot and Detached Chain Stitch. Surround each bullion knot with a detached chain stitch.

6 **Add the cattail stems and leaves.** 3 strands of DMC 469 + Split Back Stitch.

7 **Fill in the snail's body.** 3 strands of House of Embroidery Sunlight A + Chain Stitch. Make these stitches along the length of the snail body.

8 **Fill in the snail's shell.** 2 strands of House of Embroidery Sri Lanka C and 2 strands of House of Embroidery Sunlight A + Split Back Stitch. Follow the spiral with split back stitches, using one color at a time. Start with House of Embroidery Sri Lanka C around the outer edge of the shell, then use House of Embroidery Sunlight A, then alternate colors for each row until the shell is filled.

9 **Fill in the lily pad.** 2 strands of DMC 3347 + Satin Stitch. Make these stitches diagonally across the lily pad.

10 **Add the lily flower stems.** 2 strands of DMC 3347 + Split Back Stitch.

11 **Add the flower petals.** 2 strands of House of Embroidery 76 Nasturtium A + Detached Chain Stitch. Each flower is three detached chain stitches.

12 **Fill in the tall green leaves and flower stem.** 2 strands of DMC 935 + Long and Short Stitch and Split Back Stitch. Make the stitches in the leaves vertically, following the height of each leaf. Use the split back stitch to make the stem.

13 **Add the flowers.** 2 strands of DMC 3830 + French Knot and Straight Stitch. The larger round flowers are French knots, and the smaller flowers are straight stitches.

14 **Outline the toad.** 3 strands of DMC 434 + Split Back Stitch.

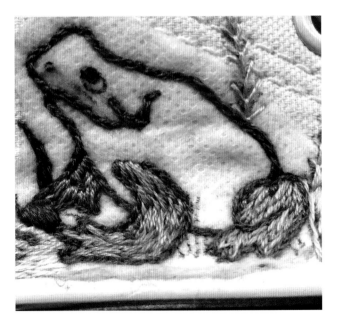

15 **Fill in the toad's legs.** 1 strand of DMC 370, 1 strand of DMC 734, and 1 strand of DMC 832 + Long and Short Satin Stitch. Follow the curves of the legs.

16 **Fill in the toad's eye and belly.** 2 strands of DMC 610 + Long and Short Satin Stitch.

17 **Fill in the toad's body.** 1 strand of DMC 370, 1 strand of DMC 734, and 1 strand of DMC 832 + French Knot. Use one thread wrap for the knots on the toad's head, then vary the number of thread wraps on the knots you use for the toad's body to create a natural, warty texture.

18 **Add the grasses around the pond.** 2 strands of DMC 319 + Split Back Stitch.

A Garden for the Bees

One of my friends is turning her yard into a pollinator garden. She wants it to be a space for bees and the plants that make them happy. After she mentioned this to me, I donated the hydrangeas in my yard to her garden. This design features a variety of flowers and mini bees flying around them.

RIGHT SHOE COLOR AND STITCH GUIDE

This diagram shows what colors and stitches are used within the design. For detailed instructions on how to create each stitch, see the Stitch Glossary starting on page 22. For the Left Shoe, see page 93.

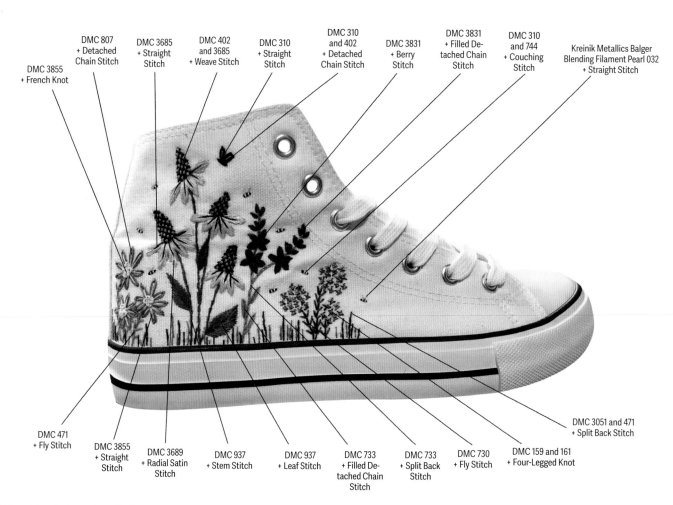

DMC 3855
+ French Knot

DMC 807
+ Detached
Chain Stitch

DMC 3685
+ Straight
Stitch

DMC 402
and 3685
+ Weave Stitch

DMC 310
+ Straight
Stitch

DMC 310
and 402
+ Detached
Chain Stitch

DMC 3831
+ Berry
Stitch

DMC 3831
+ Filled De-
tached Chain
Stitch

DMC 310
and 744
+ Couching
Stitch

Kreinik Metallics Balger
Blending Filament Pearl 032
+ Straight Stitch

DMC 471
+ Fly Stitch

DMC 3855
+ Straight
Stitch

DMC 3689
+ Radial Satin
Stitch

DMC 937
+ Stem Stitch

DMC 937
+ Leaf Stitch

DMC 733
+ Filled De-
tached Chain
Stitch

DMC 733
+ Split Back
Stitch

DMC 730
+ Fly Stitch

DMC 159 and 161
+ Four-Legged Knot

DMC 3051 and 471
+ Split Back Stitch

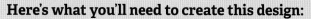

Here's what you'll need to create this design:

- Patterns (pages 126–127)
- High-top canvas shoes
- Water-soluble transfer paper or carbon paper
- Pencil or transfer pen
- Scissors

- #5 embroidery needle or darning needle
- Needle grippers
- DMC embroidery thread colors: 19, 26, 32, 159, 161, 310, 326, 335, 402, 471, 730, 733, 744, 776, 807,

937, 972, 3051, 3685, 3689, 3831, and 3855
- Kreinik Metallics Balger Blending Filament color: Pearl 032

1 **Create the hydrangea stems.** 3 strands of DMC 730 + Connected Fly Stitch.

2 **Add the hydrangea blooms.** 2 strands of DMC 159 and 2 strands of DMC 161 + Four-Legged Knot. Each flower on the hydrangea blooms is a single four-legged knot.

3 **Add the Crocosmia 'Lucifer' stem.** 3 strands of DMC 733 + Split Back Stitch.

4 **Add the leaves.** 3 strands of DMC 733 + Filled Detached Chain Stitch.

5 **Add the flowers.** 4 strands of DMC 3831 + Detached Chain Stitch and Berry Stitch. Use three detached chain stitches each to add small flowers along the ends of the stem. Use five berry stitches to add the fuller flowers to the stems.

6 **Add the coneflower stems and leaves.** 3 strands of DMC 937 + Stem Stitch and Leaf Stitch.

7 **Fill in the cones of the coneflowers.** 6 strands of DMC 402 and 6 strands of DMC 3685 + Woven/Weave Stitch. Use the 6 strands of DMC 402 to create the vertical rows of the weave stitch. Use the 6 strands of DMC 3685 to fill in the horizontal rows of the weave stitch.

8 **Fill in the coneflower petals.** 3 strands of DMC 3689 + Radial Satin Stitch.

9 **Add accent lines on the tip of each petal.** 2 strands of DMC 3685 + Straight Stitch.

10 **Add the daisy stems.** 3 strands of DMC 471 + Connected Fly Stitch.

11 **Add the daisy petals.** 3 strands of DMC 807 + Detached Chain Stitch.

12 **Fill in the daisy petals.** 3 strands of DMC 3855 + Straight Stitch. Make the stitches in the centers of the detached chain petals.

13 **Fill in the daisy centers.** 3 strands of DMC 3855 + French Knot.

14 **Add the bumblebee bodies.** 3 strands of DMC 310 and 2 strands of DMC 744 + Couching Stitch. Use DMC 310 as the laid threads DMC 744 as the tacking threads to create the bumblebee stripes.

15 **Add the bumblebee wings.** 4 strands of Kreinik Metallics Balger Blending Filament Pearl 032 + Straight Stitch. Be gentle with this thread as it can tear easily.

16 **Add the butterfly.** 3 strands of DMC 310 + Detached Chain Stitch and Straight Stitch. Use two detached chain stitches to create the wings and use a straight stitch to create the body.

17 **Fill in the butterfly wings.** 4 strands of DMC 402 + Straight Stitch.

18 **Add the grass stalks along the bottom.** 2 strands of DMC 3051 and 2 strands of DMC 471 + Split Back Stitch. Use DMC 3051 for half of the grass stalks and use DMC 471 to add the remaining stitches.

LEFT SHOE COLOR AND STITCH GUIDE

This diagram shows what colors and stitches are used within the design. For detailed instructions on how to create each stitch, see the Stitch Glossary starting on page 22. For the Right Shoe, see page 88.

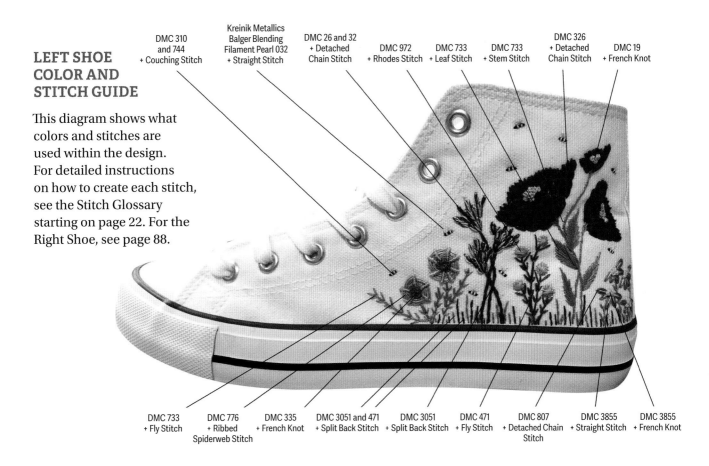

DMC 310 and 744 + Couching Stitch

Kreinik Metallics Balger Blending Filament Pearl 032 + Straight Stitch

DMC 26 and 32 + Detached Chain Stitch

DMC 972 + Rhodes Stitch

DMC 733 + Leaf Stitch

DMC 733 + Stem Stitch

DMC 326 + Detached Chain Stitch

DMC 19 + French Knot

DMC 733 + Fly Stitch

DMC 776 + Ribbed Spiderweb Stitch

DMC 335 + French Knot

DMC 3051 and 471 + Split Back Stitch

DMC 3051 + Split Back Stitch

DMC 471 + Fly Stitch

DMC 807 + Detached Chain Stitch

DMC 3855 + Straight Stitch

DMC 3855 + French Knot

INSTRUCTIONS FOR LEFT SHOE

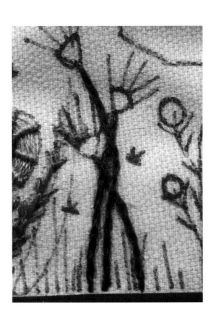

1 **Add the rose stems.** 3 strands of DMC 733 + Connected Fly Stitch.

2 **Fill in the rose blooms.** 3 strands of DMC 776 + Ribbed Spiderweb Stitch.

3 **Fill in the center of the roses.** 4 strands of DMC 335 + French Knot.

4 **Add the clover stems.** 4 strands of DMC 3051 + Split Back Stitch.

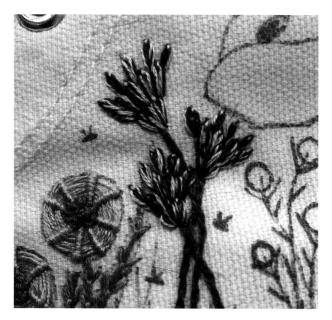

5 **Add the clover flowers.** 2 strands of DMC 26 and 2 strands of DMC 32 + Detached Chain Stitch. Start at the top of the flower and stitch in rows to the point where the flower attaches to the stem.

6 **Create the marigold blossoms.** 3 strands of DMC 972 + Rhodes Stitch.

7 **Add the marigold stems.** 3 strands of DMC 730 + Connected Fly Stitch.

8 **Add the tulip stems.** 2 strands of DMC 733 + Stem Stitch.

9 **Add the tulip leaves.** 2 strands of DMC 733 + Leaf Stitch.

10 **Fill in the tulip flowers.** 3 strands of DMC 326 + Detached Chain Stitch. Make the stitches in rows, working from the top of the petal to the bottom and slightly overlapping the bottom of the previous row with the top of the next row.

11 **Fill in the tulip centers.** 3 strands of DMC 19 + French Knot.

13 **Add the bumblebees.** Follow Right Shoe Instructions Steps 14 and 15 on page 92.

14 **Add the grass.** Follow Right Shoe Instructions Step 18 on page 92.

12 **Add the daisies.** Follow Right Shoe Instructions Steps 10–13 on pages 91–92.

Woodland Mushrooms

Thanks to the many walks my dogs and I go on around our neighborhood, I have gotten to see a variety of plants and mushrooms. This design was inspired by some of the mushrooms I've seen growing in my yard and the yards of others during our daily walks.

What you'll need to create this design:

- Pattern (page 126)
- Slip-on canvas shoes
- Water-soluble transfer paper or carbon paper
- Pencil or transfer pen
- Scissors
- Darning needle
- Needle grippers
- DMC embroidery thread colors: 22, 469, 581, 822, 936, 937, 951, 3046, 3348, and 3772

COLOR AND STITCH GUIDE

This diagram shows what colors and stitches are used within the design. For detailed instructions on how to create each stitch, see the Stitch Glossary starting on page 22.

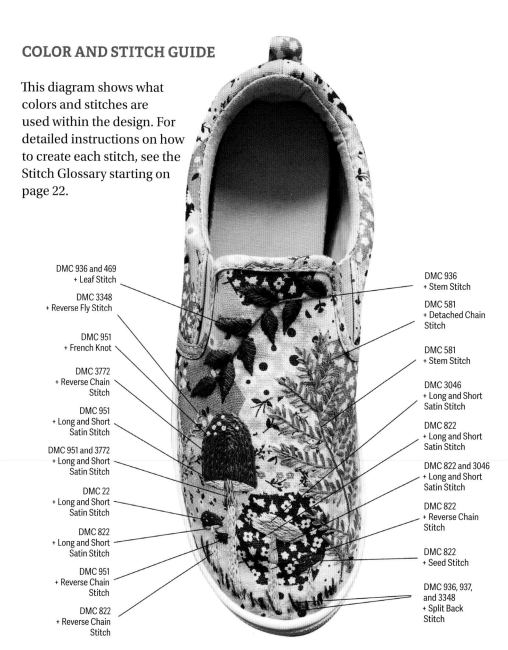

DMC 936 and 469
+ Leaf Stitch

DMC 3348
+ Reverse Fly Stitch

DMC 951
+ French Knot

DMC 3772
+ Reverse Chain Stitch

DMC 951
+ Long and Short Satin Stitch

DMC 951 and 3772
+ Long and Short Satin Stitch

DMC 22
+ Long and Short Satin Stitch

DMC 822
+ Long and Short Satin Stitch

DMC 951
+ Reverse Chain Stitch

DMC 822
+ Reverse Chain Stitch

DMC 936
+ Stem Stitch

DMC 581
+ Detached Chain Stitch

DMC 581
+ Stem Stitch

DMC 3046
+ Long and Short Satin Stitch

DMC 822
+ Long and Short Satin Stitch

DMC 822 and 3046
+ Long and Short Satin Stitch

DMC 822
+ Reverse Chain Stitch

DMC 822
+ Seed Stitch

DMC 936, 937, and 3348
+ Split Back Stitch

1 **Fill in the first mushroom cap.** 3 strands of DMC 3772 + Reverse Chain Stitch. Start along the outer edge and stitch rows in arcs toward the center of the mushroom cap.

2 **Fill in the top of the mushroom stem.** 2 strands of DMC 951 and 1 strand of DMC 3772 + Long and Short Satin Stitch. Make these stitches vertically.

3 **Fill in the underside of the mushroom cap.** 2 strands of DMC 951 + Long and Short Satin Stitch. Make these stitches horizontally and slightly overlap the bottom edge of the chain stitch rows.

4 **Add spots to the mushroom cap.** 2 strands of DMC 951 + French Knot. Add as many or as few as you'd like!

5 **Fill in the mushroom stem.** 3 strands of DMC 951 + Reverse Chain Stitch. Stitch these lines vertically.

6 **Fill in the smaller red mushroom caps.** 2 strands of DMC 22 + Long and Short Satin Stitch. Make these stitches horizontally across the caps.

7 **Fill in the undersides of the red mushroom caps.** 2 strands of DMC 822 + Long and Short Satin Stitch. Make these stitches horizontally, stitching around the stems to leave room.

8 **Fill in the mushroom stems.** 2 strands of DMC 822 + Reverse Chain Stitch. Make these stitches in vertical lines. As the section tapers off, overlap the rows slightly.

9 **Add spots to the mushroom caps.** 2 strands of DMC 822 + Seed Stitch. Scatter the stitches around the cap.

10 Fill in the last mushroom cap. 3 strands of DMC 3046 + Long and Short Satin Stitch. Make these stitches horizontally across the cap.

11 Fill in the top of the mushroom stem. 2 strands of DMC 3046 and 1 strand of DMC 822 + Long and Short Satin Stitch. Make these stitches vertically.

12 Fill in the underside of the mushroom cap. 3 strands of DMC 822 + Long and Short Satin Stitch. Make these stitches horizontally.

13 Fill in the mushroom stem. 3 strands of DMC 822 + Reverse Chain Stitch. Stitch these rows vertically. As the section tapers off, overlap the rows slightly.

14 Add the main fern stem. 2 strands of DMC 581 + Stem Stitch. Start at the base of the fern and stitch toward the shoe opening. Once the center stem is finished, knot the thread off.

15 Add the remaining fern branches and leaves. 2 strands of DMC 581 + Stem Stitch and Detached Chain Stitch. Stitch a branch stem first with the stem stitch, then add the detached chain leaves. Finish each branch before moving on to the next.

16 **Add the leafy branches.** 2 strands of DMC 3348 + Reverse Fly Stitch. Start at the top of each stem and stitch toward the toe. Knot and cut the thread after each branch to avoid creating long thread jumps on the inside of the shoe.

17 **Add the first layer of grass stalks.** 3 strands of DMC 937 + Split Back Stitch.

18 **Add the second layer of grass stalks.** 3 strands of DMC 3348 + Split Back Stitch.

19 **Add the final layer of grass stalks.** 3 strands of DMC 936 + Split Back Stitch.

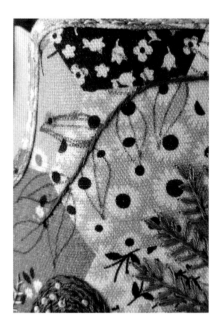

20 **Add the top branch.** 2 strands of DMC 936 + Stem Stitch.

21 **Fill in the leaves.** 1 strand of DMC 936 and 2 strands of DMC 469 + Leaf Stitch.

Under the Sea

Walking into the Seattle Aquarium almost feels like you're walking underwater. The giant glass wall of sea life is immersive and colorful. I've visited the aquarium quite a few times, and my favorite thing is the octopus that can fit into all sorts of nooks and crannies. This design plays with stump work to create additional dimension and whimsy for this dive under the sea.

What you'll need to create this design:

- Pattern (page 127)
- Boat-style canvas shoes
- Water-soluble transfer paper or carbon paper
- Scissors
- Pencil or transfer pen
- Darning needle
- Needle grippers
- Cosmo embroidery thread color: 440
- DMC embroidery thread colors: 162, 319, 349, 351, 3770, 3822, 3823, and 4150
- House of Embroidery colors: 28 Aquatic A, 49 Fuchsia A, and 76 Nasturtium A
- Felt
- Sewing pins
- 10/0 navy blue seed beads

COLOR AND STITCH GUIDE

This diagram shows what colors and stitches are used within the design. For detailed instructions on how to create each stitch, see the Stitch Glossary starting on page 22.

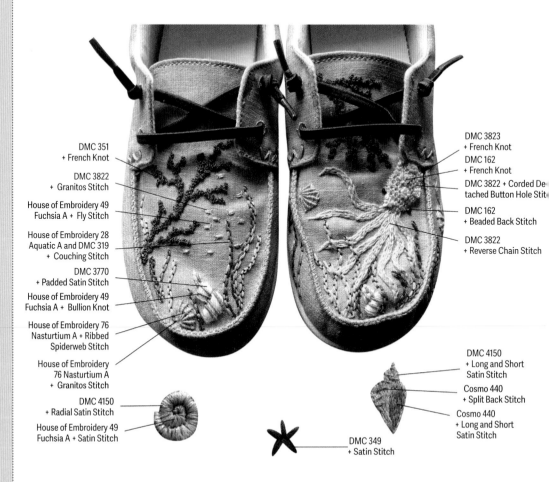

DMC 351 + French Knot

DMC 3822 + Granitos Stitch

House of Embroidery 49 Fuchsia A + Fly Stitch

House of Embroidery 28 Aquatic A and DMC 319 + Couching Stitch

DMC 3770 + Padded Satin Stitch

House of Embroidery 49 Fuchsia A + Bullion Knot

House of Embroidery 76 Nasturtium A + Ribbed Spiderweb Stitch

House of Embroidery 76 Nasturtium A + Granitos Stitch

DMC 4150 + Radial Satin Stitch

House of Embroidery 49 Fuchsia A + Satin Stitch

DMC 3823 + French Knot

DMC 162 + French Knot

DMC 3822 + Corded Detached Button Hole Stitch

DMC 162 + Beaded Back Stitch

DMC 3822 + Reverse Chain Stitch

DMC 4150 + Long and Short Satin Stitch

Cosmo 440 + Split Back Stitch

Cosmo 440 + Long and Short Satin Stitch

DMC 349 + Satin Stitch

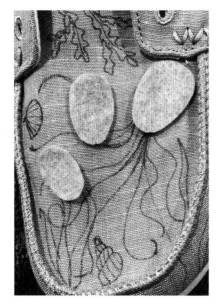  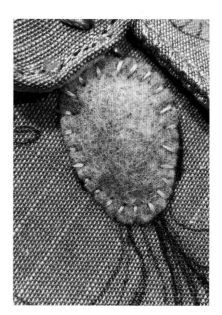

1 Create the padding for the octopus's head. Trace the head of the octopus onto a piece of felt three times. Cut out the felt. Leave one felt piece the original shape. Trim the second piece to be slightly smaller than the original, and the third to be smaller than the second.

2 Attach the first padding layer. 2 strands of DMC 3822 + Straight Stitch. Pin the largest piece of felt where you'll be stitching the octopus's head. Make short straight stitches around the outside to attach the piece of felt to the shoe. These stitches should be perpendicular to the edge of the felt and overlap the outer edge to connect it to the shoe.

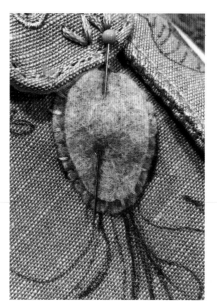 

3 Add the remaining padding layers. 2 strands of DMC 3822 + Straight Stitch. Repeat Step 2 to add the second and third pieces of felt on top of the first piece. Add a final straight stitch in the center.

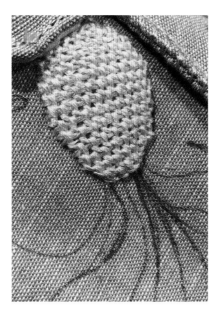
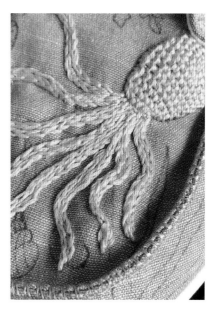

4 **Fill in the octopus's head.** 6 strands of DMC 3822 + Corded Detached Buttonhole Stitch.

5 **Add the octopus's arms.** 6 strands of DMC 3822 + Reverse Chain Stitch. Start each arm by stitching into the base of the octopus's head. Each arm is two rows of reverse chain stitches that taper off at the ends. Stitch over the seaweed lines.

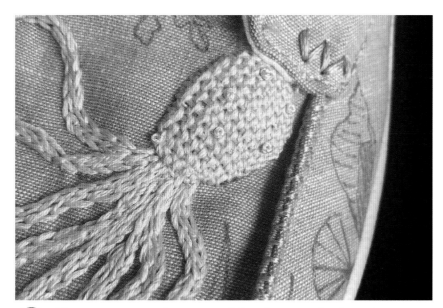

6 **Add spot centers to the octopus's head.** 3 strands of DMC 162 + French Knot. Each French knot is made with three thread wraps around the needle. Add as many or as few spots as you'd like!

7 **Finish the octopus's spots.** 3 strands of DMC 3823 + French Knot. Add French knots in circles around the French knots you made in Step 6.

8 **Add the tops of the clam shells.** 3 strands of House of Embroidery 76 Nasturtium A + Ribbed Spiderweb Stitch. Because the shell is only a section of the usual ribbed spiderweb stitch's circle, the last weave at the edge of the shell will be a single strand. At the edge of each row, bring the needle back down through the shoe and start again on the opposite side. As the shell starts to taper off, skip the finished straight stitch and use the outer edge of the shell as a guide for starting each new row.

9 **Add the bases of the clam shells.** 3 strands of House of Embroidery 76 Nasturtium A + Granitos Stitch

10 **Add the layers of the Babylon shell.** 4 strands of DMC 3770 + Padded Satin Stitch.

11 **Add the ridges.** 2 strands House of Embroidery 49 Fuschia A + Bullion Knot. Overlay the padded satin stitch sections with the bullion knots. These bullion knots will start at the base of each shell section and end at the top, creating three vertical rows of knots on the bottom level, two vertical rows on the second level, and one vertical row on the third level.

12 **Add the coral.** 2 strands of DMC 351 + French Knot. Fill in the shape with knots. Each French knot is made with two wraps of thread.

13 **Add the starfish.** 3 strands of DMC 349 + Satin Stitch.

14 **Add the spiral shell.** 3 strands of DMC 4150 + Radial Satin Stitch. Make these stitches using short stitches that follow the spiral of the shell.

16 **Add detail lines to the spiral shell.** 2 strands of House of Embroidery 49 Fuchsia A + Satin Stitch. These stitches start at the inner spiral edge and should be about half the width of the spiral shell section. Add as many or as few as you'd like.

17 **Fill the outer section of the conch shell.** 3 strands of DMC 4150 + Long and Short Satin Stitch. Make these stitches vertically.

18 **Fill the inside of the conch shell.** 3 strands of Cosmo 440 + Long and Short Satin Stitch. Make these stitches vertically.

19 **Add detail lines to the conch shell.** 2 strands of Cosmo 440 + Split Back Stitch.

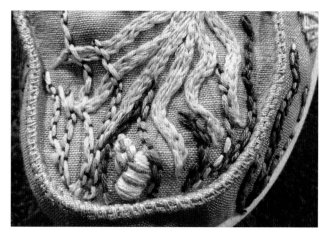

20 **Add the seaweed.** 6 strands of House of Embroidery 28 Aquatic A and 2 strands of DMC 319 + Couching Stitch. Use House of Embroidery 28 Aquatic A as the laid threads and DMC 319 as the tacking threads. Each strand of seaweed is two to three rows of couched thread. Work the thread on the top of the shoe, creating each strand of seaweed one at a time. At the end of the seaweed, cut the laid thread on the front of the shoe, ensuring that it's couched tightly to the shoe.

21 Add the octopus's eyes. 2 strands of DMC 162 + Beaded Seed Stitch. Use one bead on each side of the octopus's head. Knot the thread after each eye to secure it on the back.

RIGHT SHOE INSTRUCTIONS

1 Add the seaweed, coral, and shells. Use the same stitches and thread colors that you used for the right shoe.

2 Add the fish bodies. 3 strands of DMC 3822 + Granitos Stitch.

3 Add the fish fins. 2 strands of House of Embroidery 49 Fuchsia A + Connected Fly Stitch.

Ladybug Fern Espadrilles

Ferns grow aplenty in the Pacific Northwest. I often see them while on walks with my dogs. My little boy pup, Landen, loves to try to eat any bugs he finds while we're out—even little ladybugs! This design lets you build your own pattern of ferns and ladybugs to create a unique pair of shoes. You can add this design to any type of shoe, but I've paired it with homemade, custom espadrilles for a truly one-of-a-kind project! See page 118 for instructions on how to make your own espadrilles.

COLOR AND STITCH GUIDE

This diagram shows what colors and stitches are used within the design. For detailed instructions on how to create each stitch, see the Stitch Glossary starting on page 22.

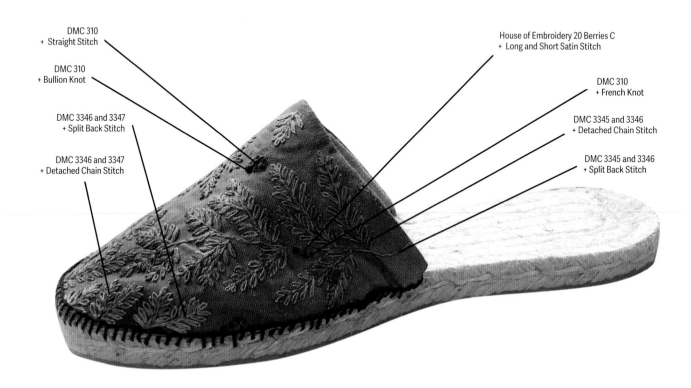

DMC 310
+ Straight Stitch

DMC 310
+ Bullion Knot

DMC 3346 and 3347
+ Split Back Stitch

DMC 3346 and 3347
+ Detached Chain Stitch

House of Embroidery 20 Berries C
+ Long and Short Satin Stitch

DMC 310
+ French Knot

DMC 3345 and 3346
+ Detached Chain Stitch

DMC 3345 and 3346
+ Split Back Stitch

What you'll need to create this design:

- Patterns (page 124)
- ¼ yd. (22.9cm) fabric in chosen color for outside of shoe
- ¼ yd. (22.9cm) fabric in chosen color for inside of shoe
- Espadrille soles
- Water-soluble transfer paper
- Transfer pen or pencil
- Small, sharp scissors
- Fabric scissors
- Paper scissors
- 5" (12.7cm) embroidery hoop
- Darning needle
- Needle grippers
- Chopstick or similar tool
- Sewing pins or clips
- Iron and ironing board
- DMC embroidery thread colors: 310, 3334, 3345, 3346, and 3347
- House of Embroidery thread color: 20 Berries C
- Sewing machine (optional, but will make the process much quicker)
- Sewing thread in the same color as the outside fabric

INSTRUCTIONS

1 Follow the espadrille fabric preparation steps (Steps 1–4) starting on page 118. **Note:** If you are creating slides, do not use the heel pattern. For Step 4, arrange the ferns and ladybugs on the fabric in the arrangement you like most.

2 Place the fabric in the embroidery hoop.

3 Add the darker ferns. 1 strand of DMC 3345 and 1 strand of DMC 3346 + Split Back Stitch and Detached Chain Stitch. Use the split back stitch to create the center line. Then, working one branch at a time, use the split back stitch to create the smaller branches and the detached chain stitch to add leaves.

4 **Add the lighter ferns.** 1 strand of DMC 3346 and 1 strand of DMC 3347+ Split Back Stitch and Detached Chain Stitch. Stitch these ferns the same way you made the ferns in Step 3.

5 **Add the ladybugs.** 2 strands of House of Embroidery 20 Berries C + Long and Short Satin Stitch and Satin Stitch. Place full ladybugs to the spaces around the ferns using the long and short satin stitch to fill in the bodies. Place side-view ladybugs next to the fern stems using satin stitches that are perpendicular to the stem.

6 **Add the heads to the ladybugs.** 2 strands of DMC 310 + French Knot and Bullion Knot. The side-view ladybugs have French knots for heads and the full ladybugs have bullion knots for heads.

7 **Add the spots to the ladybugs.** 1 strand of DMC 310 + French knot. Add as many or as few spots to the ladybugs' bodies as you'd like.

8 **Finish the full ladybugs.** 1 strand of DMC 310 + Straight Stitch. Make the straight stitch down the center of the red body.

9 **Follow the remaining espadrille instructions, starting with Step 6 on page 119.**

Tropical Plants Espadrilles

When my husband and I travel together, we love to visit warm destinations. We're often craving tropical weather and vibrant plants during those dreary and rainy winter months. This design was inspired by some of the lush plants we've seen on our travels. You can add this design to any type of shoe, but I've paired it with homemade, custom espadrilles for a truly one-of-a-kind project! See page 118 for instructions on how to make your own espadrilles.

What you'll need to create this design:

- Pattern (page 126)
- ¼ yd. (22.9cm) fabric in chosen color for outside of shoe
- ¼ yd. (22.9cm) fabric in chosen color for inside of shoe
- Espadrille soles
- Water-soluble transfer paper
- Transfer pen or pencil
- Small, sharp scissors
- Fabric scissors

- Paper scissors
- 5" (12.7cm) embroidery hoop
- Darning needle
- Needle grippers
- Chopstick or similar tool
- Sewing pins or clips
- Iron and ironing board
- DMC embroidery thread colors: 335, 890, 897, and 987

- House of Embroidery thread color: 6 Privet A
- Sulky 12-wt. Cotton Petites Art thread color: 712-1177
- Sulky 12-wt. Cotton Blendables thread color: 712-4030
- Sewing machine (optional, but will make the process much quicker)
- Sewing thread in the same color as the outside fabric

COLOR AND STITCH GUIDE

This diagram shows what colors and stitches are used within the design. For detailed instructions on how to create each stitch, see the Stitch Glossary starting on page 22.

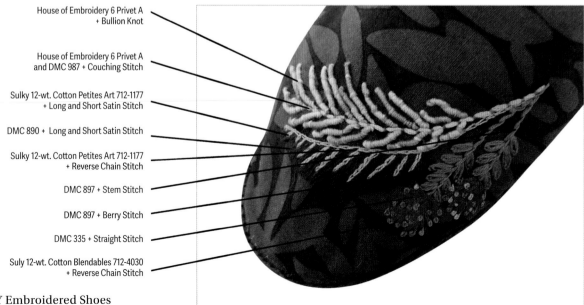

House of Embroidery 6 Privet A + Bullion Knot

House of Embroidery 6 Privet A and DMC 987 + Couching Stitch

Sulky 12-wt. Cotton Petites Art 712-1177 + Long and Short Satin Stitch

DMC 890 + Long and Short Satin Stitch

Sulky 12-wt. Cotton Petites Art 712-1177 + Reverse Chain Stitch

DMC 897 + Stem Stitch

DMC 897 + Berry Stitch

DMC 335 + Straight Stitch

Suly 12-wt. Cotton Blendables 712-4030 + Reverse Chain Stitch

INSTRUCTIONS

1 Follow the espadrille fabric preparation steps (Steps 1–4) starting on page 118. **Note:** If you are creating slides, do not use the heel pattern. For Step 4, be sure to mirror the pattern appropriately for the right and left shoes.

2 Place the fabric in the embroidery hoop.

3 Add the protea stems. 3 strands of DMC 987 + Stem Stitch.

4 Add leaves to the stems. 2 strands of DMC 987 + Berry Stitch.

5 Fill in the protea blooms. 4 strands of DMC 335 + Straight Stitch.

6 Add dot details to the protea flowers. 1 strand of Sulky 12-wt. Cotton Blendables 712-4030 + French Knot. These French knots should be made at the top of each of the straight stitches made in Step 5.

7 Add the palm leaf stem. 2 strands of Sulky 12-wt. Cotton Petites Art 712-1177 + Reverse Chain Stitch.

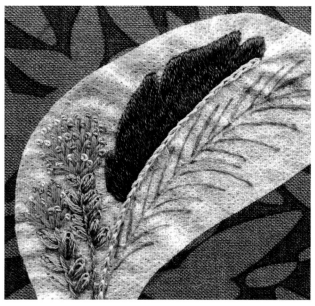

8 **Fill in the palm leaf.** 2 strands of DMC 890 + Long and Short Satin Stitch. Make these stitches across the width of the leaf.

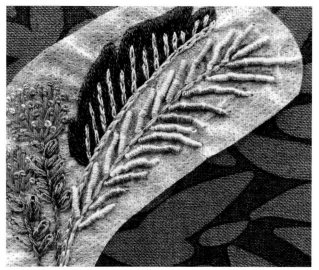

9 **Add accent lines to the palm leaf.** 1 strand of Sulky 12-wt. Cotton Petites Art 712-1177 + Chain Stitch.

10 **Create the fern stem.** 6 strands of House of Embroidery 6 Privet A and 2 strands of DMC 987 + Couching Stitch. Use House of Embroidery 6 Privet A as the laid threads and DMC 987 as the tacking threads.

11 **Add the fern leaves.** 3 strands of House of Embroidery 6 Privet A + Bullion Knot. To ensure that the bullion knots lay flat to the fabric, couch them with a few small stitches once they're stitched.

12 **Follow the remaining espadrille instructions, starting with Step 6 on page 119.**

Bonus Project: Create Your Own Espadrilles

You can sew your own pair of shoes! Espadrilles are shoes you can sew together with your favorite fabrics, then easily add the soles. This is a fun and easy way to create your own custom footwear. This bonus project lays out the basic materials and steps to help you get started sewing. The two espadrille projects (pages 110 and 114) are designed specifically to be added to this type of shoe, but you can use any of the designs in the book! Simply use these steps and sub in your favorite design, embroidering it on the fabric prior to shoe construction.

What you'll need to create your own espadrilles:

- Patterns (toe and heel patterns on page 128; embroidery designs starting on page 122)
- ¼ yd. (22.9cm) fabric in chosen color for outside of shoe
- ¼ yd. (22.9cm) fabric in chosen color for inside of shoe
- Espadrille soles
- Water-soluble transfer paper

- Transfer pen or pencil
- Small, sharp scissors
- Fabric scissors
- Paper scissors
- Darning needle
- Needle grippers
- Chopstick or similar tool
- Sewing pins or clips

- Iron and ironing board
- Embroidery thread
- Sewing machine (optional, but will make the process much quicker)
- Sewing thread in the same color as the outside fabric

INSTRUCTIONS

1 **Wash both fabrics.** This will prevent fabric shrinkage.

2 **Determine your shoe size and make the patterns.** Print the pattern template at 100% scale, then cut out the pattern size you need. If you're not sure if your pattern is printed to scale, measure the square box. Make sure it measures 1" x 1" (2.5 x 2.5cm) before you place and cut your pieces, or your finished shoes will be the wrong size.

3 **Iron both fabrics.**

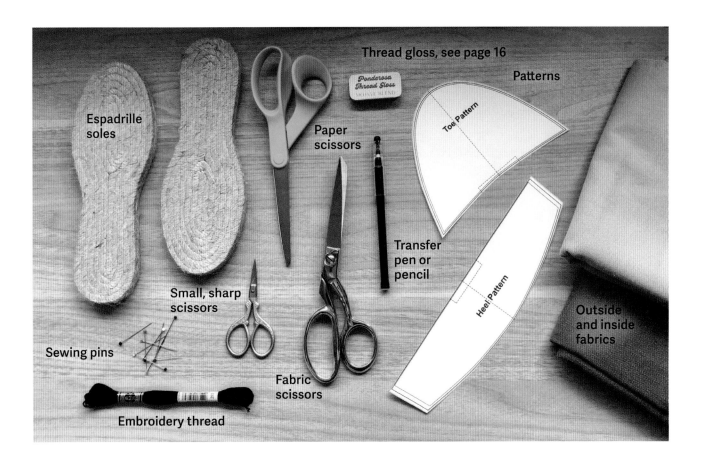

Espadrille soles

Thread gloss, see page 16

Ponderosa Thread Gloss

Patterns

Paper scissors

Toe Pattern

Transfer pen or pencil

Small, sharp scissors

Heel Pattern

Outside and inside fabrics

Sewing pins

Fabric scissors

Embroidery thread

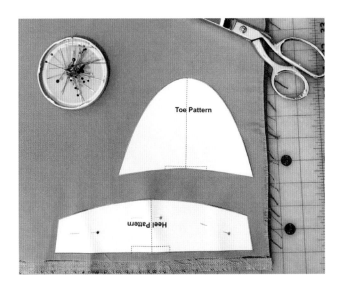

Toe Pattern

Heel Pattern

5 **Embroider the outside fabric.** If you are planning to embroider your espadrilles, follow the instructions in the specific embroidery project. If you are using a design originally stitched on a finished shoe, simply place your fabric in an embroidery hoop and embroider the design as usual (see pages 112 and 116 if you need more detail). If you are making plain espadrilles, skip to Step 7.

6 **Wash away the stabilizer.** After the design is embroidered, wash away the stabilizer by running the fabric under warm to hot water. This should dissolve the pattern. If there is some residue left, gently agitate the pattern with your fingers under the water to scrub away any additional stabilizer. Lay the fabric flat to dry.

4 **Lay both fabrics on a flat surface and transfer the patterns.** Use the transfer pen to trace one set (two each) of both the toe and heal patterns on each fabric. Leave at least a 1" (2.5cm) of space between each pattern piece to allow for seam allowances. **Note:** If you want to make slides instead of full shoes, only trace the toe patterns.

7 **Add the seam allowances.** Trace a ¼" (6.4mm) outline around each pattern piece. **Note:** If you embroidered the fabric and washed away the stabilizer, you may need to retrace the toe or heel pattern outlines before adding the seam allowances.

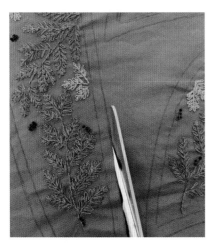

8 Cut out the patterns along the seam allowance line.

9 Pin or clip the right sides of the fabrics together. Pin the toe pieces together and pin the heal pieces together.

10 Sew the inside and outside fabric pieces together. Use a sewing machine and a ¼" (6.4mm) seam allowance to sew the inside and outside fabrics of each piece together. Leave a ½" (1.3cm) opening on each pattern piece so they can be flipped right side out. **Note:** If you don't have a sewing machine, you can use the split back stitch to sew the pieces together. I recommend marking the stitch line on the fabric to keep your handsewn lines straight.

11 Trim the corners diagonally to eliminate bulk.

12 Flip the pieces right side out. Insert a chopstick or similar tool into the seam openings to gently poke the corners into crisp points. Be sure not to use anything too sharp to avoid damaging the fabric.

13 Iron the pieces flat. If you embroidered the outside of your shoes, be sure to iron with the lining up so you're not ironing directly onto your embroidery.

14 Sew the seam openings closed. Use a thread color similar to the outside fabric color with a ladder stitch. **Note:** If you are making slides instead of full shoes, skip to Step 17 and follow the instructions for the toe section.

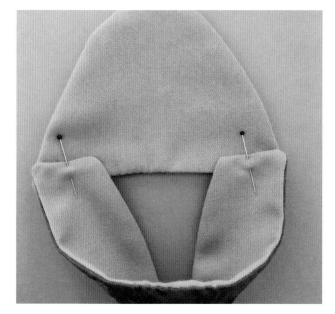

15 **Pin the toe and heel pieces together.** Lay the toe piece with the lining facing up. Align the embroidered edges of the heel to the corners of the inside of the toe piece. Overlap the pieces by ¼" (6.4mm) and pin them together.

16 **Sew the toe and heel sections together.** Use a sewing machine to sew a small rectangle as shown. **Note:** If you don't have a sewing machine, you can use the split back stitch for this part, as well.

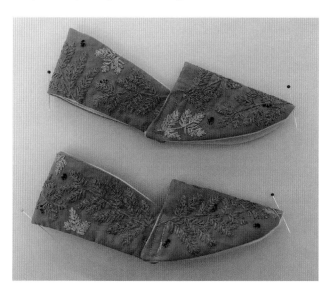

17 **Fold the shoes in half.** Mark the middle heel and toe points with sewing pins. Mark the middle heel and toe points on the espadrille soles with sewing pins, as well.

18 **Align the middle toe and heal points of the fabric pieces and the espadrille soles.** Pin the fabric to the sole. Continue pinning the fabric to the top of the shoe shole. Be sure to evenly distribute the fabric around the sole.

19 **Stitch the fabric pieces to the soles.** 6 strands chosen embroidery thread + Blanket Stitch. Hide the knot inside the shoe near the seam. Your stitches should be about ¼" (6.4mm) apart to ensure that the fabric is securely attached. After the fabric is attached, bring the needle and thread back to the inside of the shoe and knot the thread near the sole.

20 **Wear and enjoy your new shoes!**

Project Patterns

Unless otherwise noted, these patterns are included at full size. Copy them at 100% or the percentage noted to match my projects. You may need to resize the images depending on the size and style of shoe you are working with.

Scan the QR code or visit foxpatterns.com/diy-embroidered-shoes to download the Project Patterns and Additional Designs on pages 122–142.

Colorful Clouds, page 46

Photocopy at 150%

Orcas, page 50

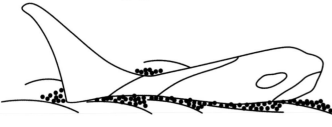

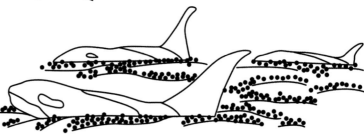

Moonlit Forest, page 54

Slither By, page 58

Mountain Sunset, page 62

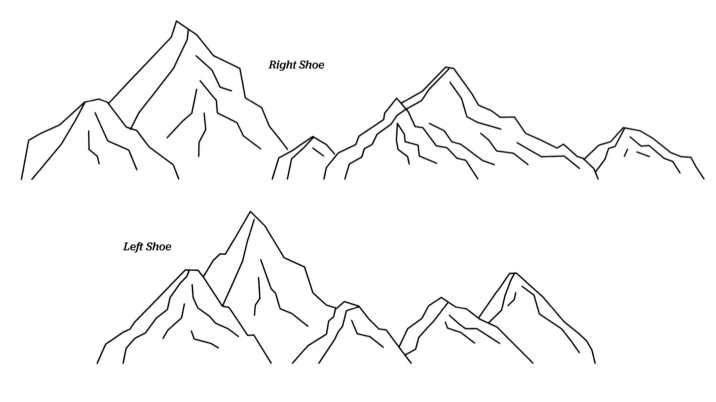

Right Shoe

Left Shoe

Ladybug Fern Espadrilles, page 110

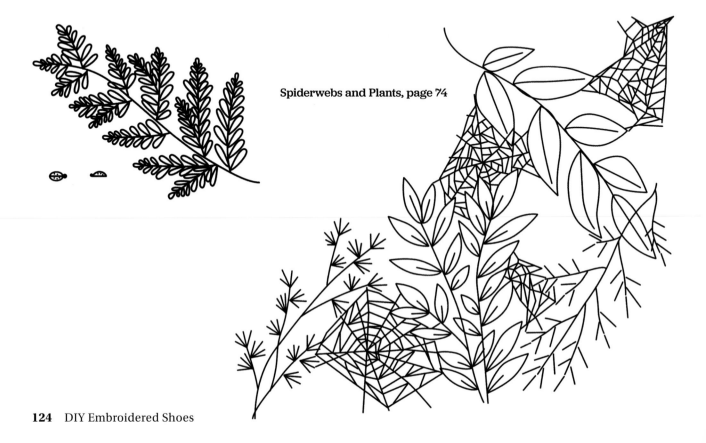

Spiderwebs and Plants, page 74

Southwest Dream, page 78

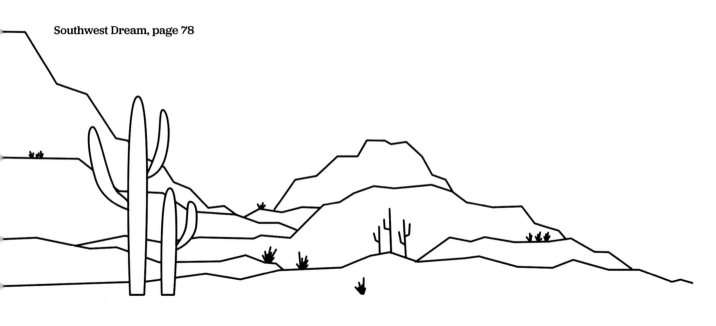

Spring Bird, page 66

Strawberry Delight, page 70

Pond Life, page 82

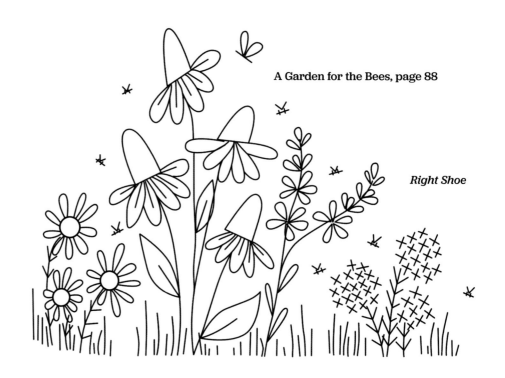

A Garden for the Bees, page 88

Right Shoe

Tropical Plants Espadrilles, page 114

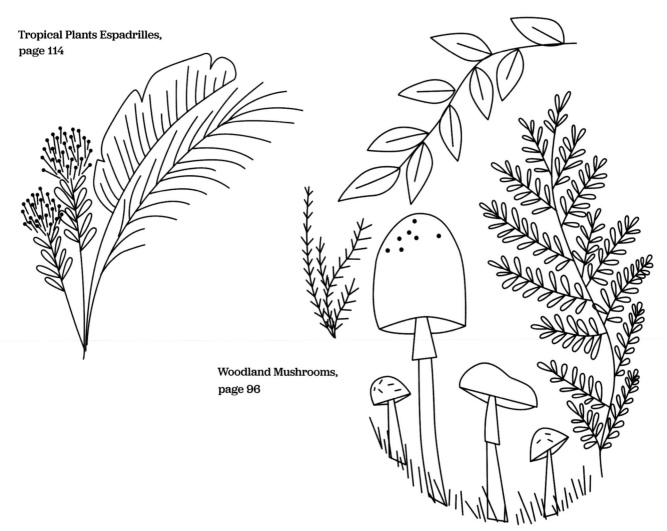

Woodland Mushrooms, page 96

Left Shoe

Under the Sea, page 102

Photocopy at 150%

Right Shoe

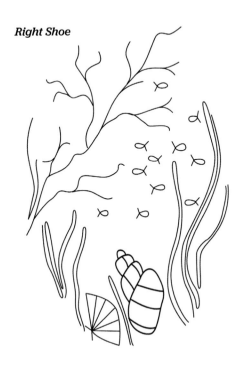

Left Shoe

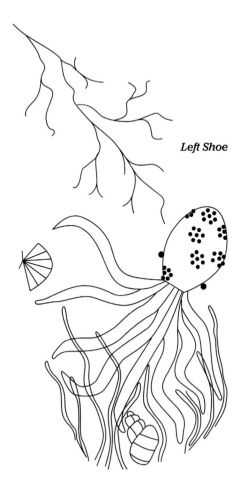

Sides

ESPADRILLE PATTERN

Bonus Project: Create Your Own Espadrilles, page 118

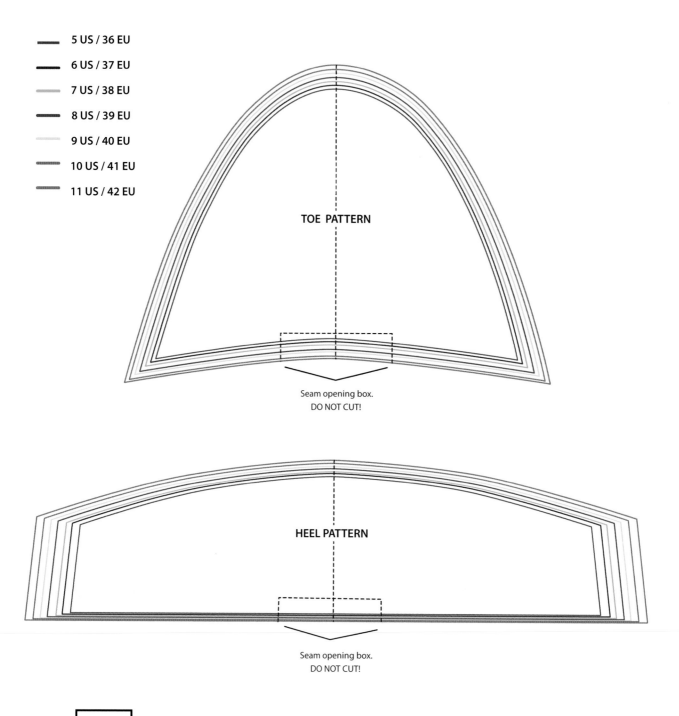

- **5 US / 36 EU**
- **6 US / 37 EU**
- **7 US / 38 EU**
- **8 US / 39 EU**
- **9 US / 40 EU**
- **10 US / 41 EU**
- **11 US / 42 EU**

TOE PATTERN

Seam opening box.
DO NOT CUT!

HEEL PATTERN

Seam opening box.
DO NOT CUT!

1" x 1"
(2.5 x 2.5cm)

When printing this pattern,
print it to 167% scale.
This square should
measure 1" x 1" (2.5 x 2.5cm)

Additional Designs

Mix and match any of these additional designs and use the skills you've developed to personalize every step you take with custom embroidery! I've included color and stitch guides for these designs, as well, but feel free to great creative. You can copy them at 100% or resize them to suit larger or smaller projects.

LETTERS AND NUMBERS

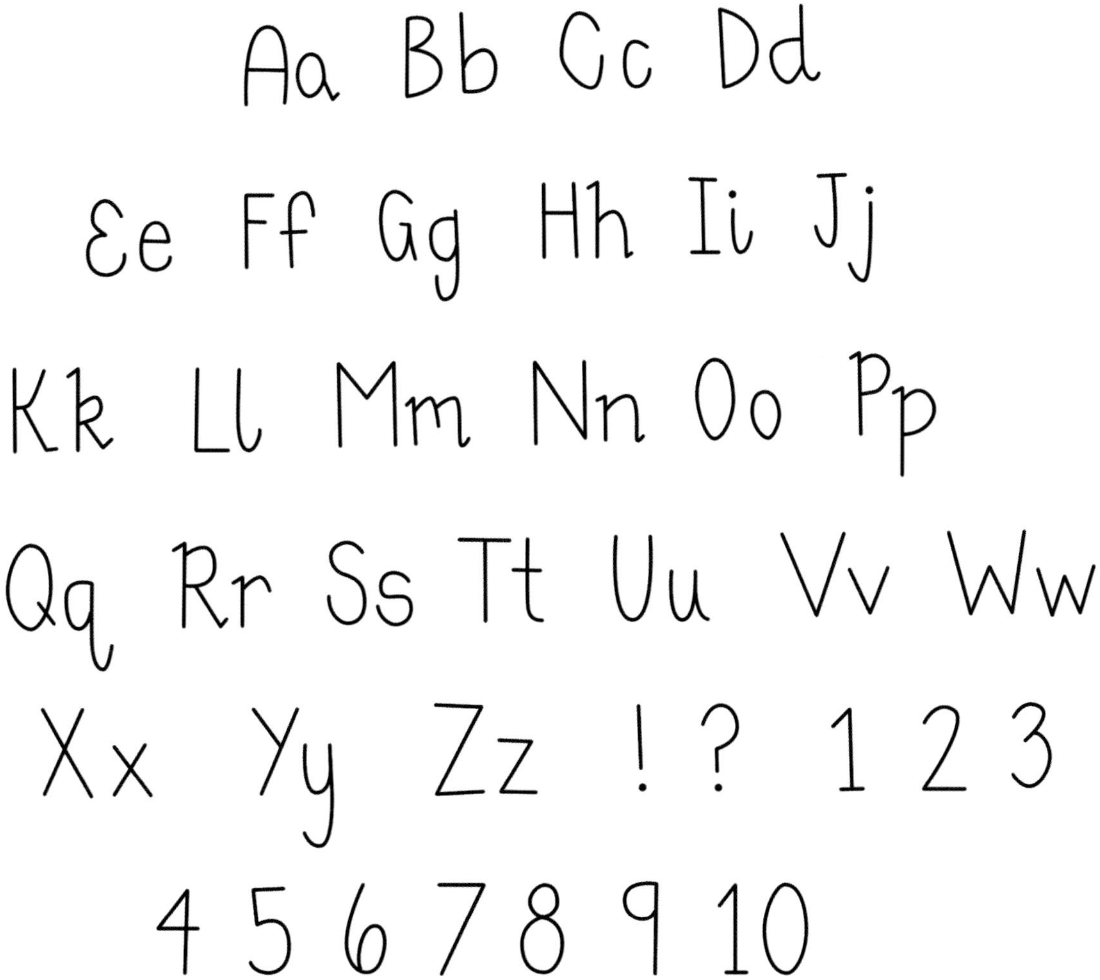

Aa Bb Cc Dd

Ee Ff Gg Hh Ii Jj

Kk Ll Mm Nn Oo Pp

Qq Rr Ss Tt Uu Vv Ww

Xx Yy Zz ! ? 1 2 3

4 5 6 7 8 9 10

Recommended embroidery stitches for lettering: back stitch, split back stitch, chain stitch, reverse chain stitch, or stem stitch.

BIRDS

Blue Jay

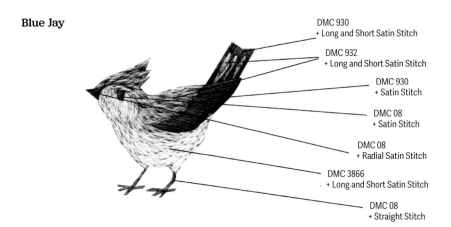

DMC 930
+ Long and Short Satin Stitch

DMC 932
+ Long and Short Satin Stitch

DMC 930
+ Satin Stitch

DMC 08
+ Satin Stitch

DMC 08
+ Radial Satin Stitch

DMC 3866
+ Long and Short Satin Stitch

DMC 08
+ Straight Stitch

Gray and Yellow Bird

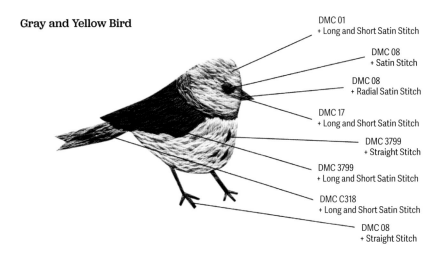

DMC 01
+ Long and Short Satin Stitch

DMC 08
+ Satin Stitch

DMC 08
+ Radial Satin Stitch

DMC 17
+ Long and Short Satin Stitch

DMC 3799
+ Straight Stitch

DMC 3799
+ Long and Short Satin Stitch

DMC C318
+ Long and Short Satin Stitch

DMC 08
+ Straight Stitch

Cardinal

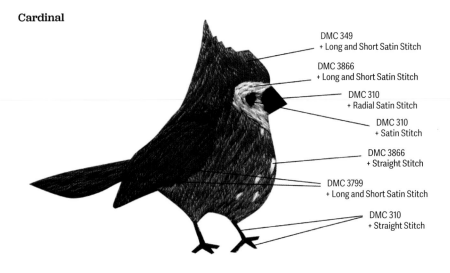

DMC 349
+ Long and Short Satin Stitch

DMC 3866
+ Long and Short Satin Stitch

DMC 310
+ Radial Satin Stitch

DMC 310
+ Satin Stitch

DMC 3866
+ Straight Stitch

DMC 3799
+ Long and Short Satin Stitch

DMC 310
+ Straight Stitch

BUGS

Beetle

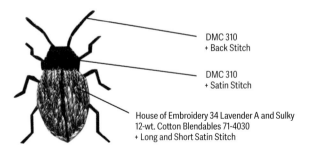

DMC 310
+ Back Stitch

DMC 310
+ Satin Stitch

House of Embroidery 34 Lavender A and Sulky
12-wt. Cotton Blendables 71-4030
+ Long and Short Satin Stitch

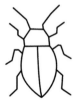

Bumblebee

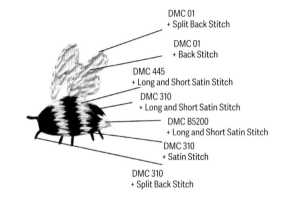

DMC 01
+ Split Back Stitch

DMC 01
+ Back Stitch

DMC 445
+ Long and Short Satin Stitch

DMC 310
+ Long and Short Satin Stitch

DMC B5200
+ Long and Short Satin Stitch

DMC 310
+ Satin Stitch

DMC 310
+ Split Back Stitch

Butterfly

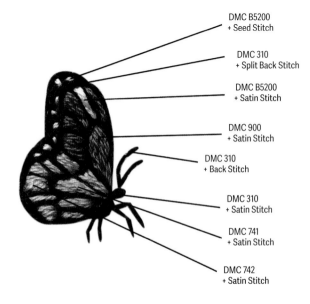

DMC B5200
+ Seed Stitch

DMC 310
+ Split Back Stitch

DMC B5200
+ Satin Stitch

DMC 900
+ Satin Stitch

DMC 310
+ Back Stitch

DMC 310
+ Satin Stitch

DMC 741
+ Satin Stitch

DMC 742
+ Satin Stitch

Caterpillar

DMC 581
+ Satin Stitch

DMC 816
+ Satin Stitch

DMC 816
+ Straight Stitch

Dragonfly

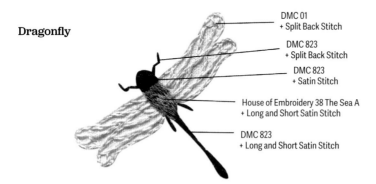

DMC 01
+ Split Back Stitch

DMC 823
+ Split Back Stitch

DMC 823
+ Satin Stitch

House of Embroidery 38 The Sea A
+ Long and Short Satin Stitch

DMC 823
+ Long and Short Satin Stitch

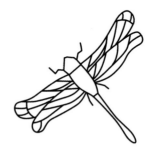

Ladybug

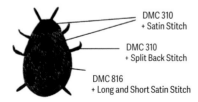

DMC 310
+ Satin Stitch

DMC 310
+ Split Back Stitch

DMC 816
+ Long and Short Satin Stitch

Worm

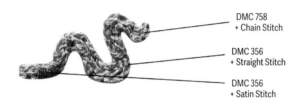

DMC 758
+ Chain Stitch

DMC 356
+ Straight Stitch

DMC 356
+ Satin Stitch

FLOWERS

Iris

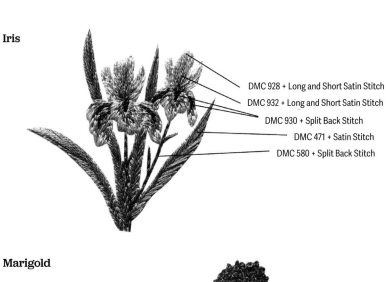

DMC 928 + Long and Short Satin Stitch
DMC 932 + Long and Short Satin Stitch
DMC 930 + Split Back Stitch
DMC 471 + Satin Stitch
DMC 580 + Split Back Stitch

Marigold

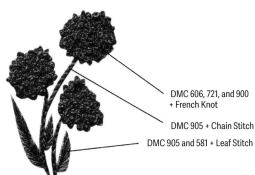

DMC 606, 721, and 900 + French Knot
DMC 905 + Chain Stitch
DMC 905 and 581 + Leaf Stitch

Pansy

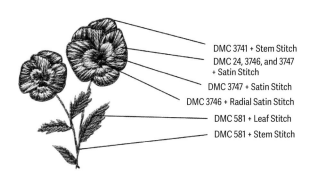

DMC 3741 + Stem Stitch
DMC 24, 3746, and 3747 + Satin Stitch
DMC 3747 + Satin Stitch
DMC 3746 + Radial Satin Stitch
DMC 581 + Leaf Stitch
DMC 581 + Stem Stitch

Spiked Protea

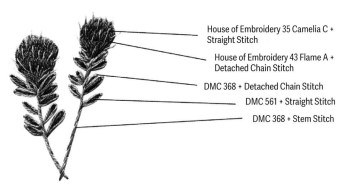
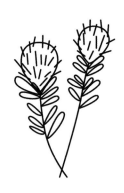

House of Embroidery 35 Camelia C + Straight Stitch
House of Embroidery 43 Flame A + Detached Chain Stitch
DMC 368 + Detached Chain Stitch
DMC 561 + Straight Stitch
DMC 368 + Stem Stitch

Apples

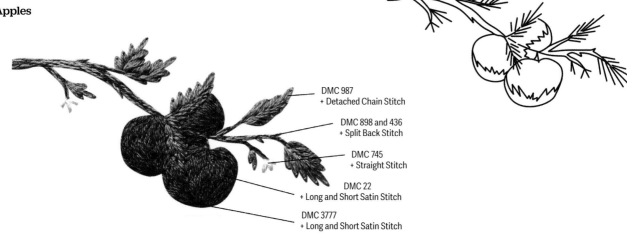

DMC 987
+ Detached Chain Stitch

DMC 898 and 436
+ Split Back Stitch

DMC 745
+ Straight Stitch

DMC 22
+ Long and Short Satin Stitch

DMC 3777
+ Long and Short Satin Stitch

Blackberries

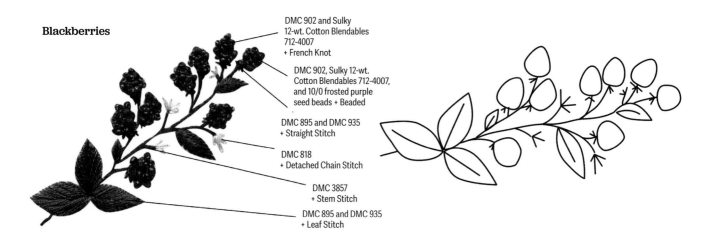

DMC 902 and Sulky
12-wt. Cotton Blendables
712-4007
+ French Knot

DMC 902, Sulky 12-wt.
Cotton Blendables 712-4007,
and 10/0 frosted purple
seed beads + Beaded

DMC 895 and DMC 935
+ Straight Stitch

DMC 818
+ Detached Chain Stitch

DMC 3857
+ Stem Stitch

DMC 895 and DMC 935
+ Leaf Stitch

Blueberries

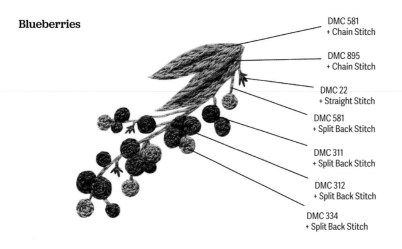

DMC 581
+ Chain Stitch

DMC 895
+ Chain Stitch

DMC 22
+ Straight Stitch

DMC 581
+ Split Back Stitch

DMC 311
+ Split Back Stitch

DMC 312
+ Split Back Stitch

DMC 334
+ Split Back Stitch

MOTHS

Brown Moth

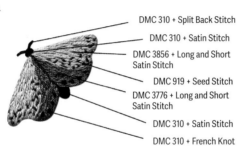

DMC 310 + Split Back Stitch
DMC 310 + Satin Stitch
DMC 3856 + Long and Short Satin Stitch
DMC 919 + Seed Stitch
DMC 3776 + Long and Short Satin Stitch
DMC 310 + Satin Stitch
DMC 310 + French Knot

Green Moth

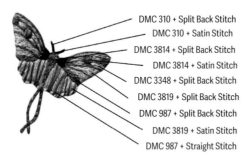

DMC 310 + Split Back Stitch
DMC 310 + Satin Stitch
DMC 3814 + Split Back Stitch
DMC 3814 + Satin Stitch
DMC 3348 + Split Back Stitch
DMC 3819 + Split Back Stitch
DMC 987 + Split Back Stitch
DMC 3819 + Satin Stitch
DMC 987 + Straight Stitch

Purple Moth

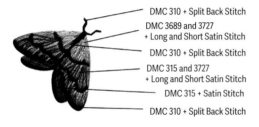

DMC 310 + Split Back Stitch
DMC 3689 and 3727 + Long and Short Satin Stitch
DMC 310 + Split Back Stitch
DMC 315 and 3727 + Long and Short Satin Stitch
DMC 315 + Satin Stitch
DMC 310 + Split Back Stitch

Red Moth

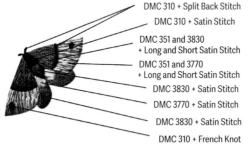

DMC 310 + Split Back Stitch
DMC 310 + Satin Stitch
DMC 351 and 3830 + Long and Short Satin Stitch
DMC 351 and 3770 + Long and Short Satin Stitch
DMC 3830 + Satin Stitch
DMC 3770 + Satin Stitch
DMC 3830 + Satin Stitch
DMC 310 + French Knot

Yellow Moth

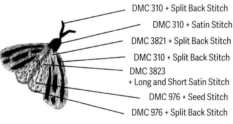

DMC 310 + Split Back Stitch
DMC 310 + Satin Stitch
DMC 3821 + Split Back Stitch
DMC 310 + Split Back Stitch
DMC 3823 + Long and Short Satin Stitch
DMC 976 + Seed Stitch
DMC 976 + Split Back Stitch

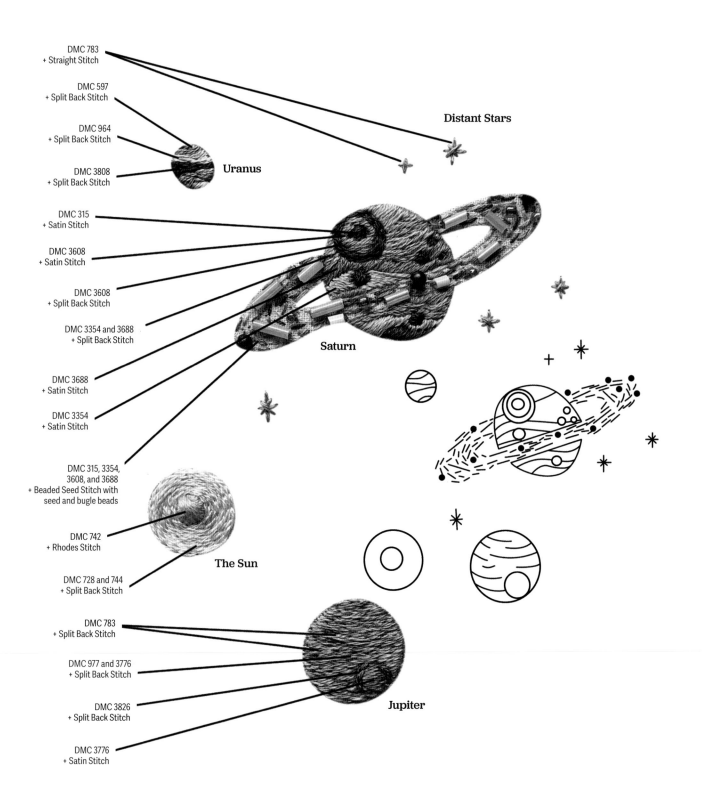

DMC 783
+ Straight Stitch

DMC 597
+ Split Back Stitch

DMC 964
+ Split Back Stitch

DMC 3808
+ Split Back Stitch

Uranus

Distant Stars

DMC 315
+ Satin Stitch

DMC 3608
+ Satin Stitch

DMC 3608
+ Split Back Stitch

DMC 3354 and 3688
+ Split Back Stitch

DMC 3688
+ Satin Stitch

DMC 3354
+ Satin Stitch

Saturn

DMC 315, 3354,
3608, and 3688
+ Beaded Seed Stitch with
seed and bugle beads

DMC 742
+ Rhodes Stitch

The Sun

DMC 728 and 744
+ Split Back Stitch

DMC 783
+ Split Back Stitch

DMC 977 and 3776
+ Split Back Stitch

DMC 3826
+ Split Back Stitch

Jupiter

DMC 3776
+ Satin Stitch

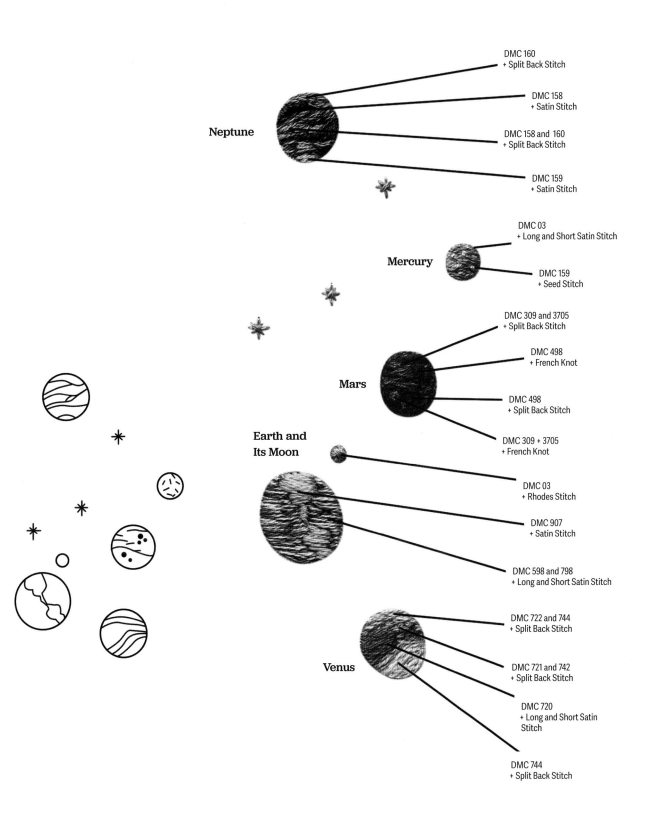

Neptune

DMC 160
+ Split Back Stitch

DMC 158
+ Satin Stitch

DMC 158 and 160
+ Split Back Stitch

DMC 159
+ Satin Stitch

Mercury

DMC 03
+ Long and Short Satin Stitch

DMC 159
+ Seed Stitch

Mars

DMC 309 and 3705
+ Split Back Stitch

DMC 498
+ French Knot

DMC 498
+ Split Back Stitch

DMC 309 + 3705
+ French Knot

**Earth and
Its Moon**

DMC 03
+ Rhodes Stitch

DMC 907
+ Satin Stitch

DMC 598 and 798
+ Long and Short Satin Stitch

Venus

DMC 722 and 744
+ Split Back Stitch

DMC 721 and 742
+ Split Back Stitch

DMC 720
+ Long and Short Satin
Stitch

DMC 744
+ Split Back Stitch

Milky Way Galaxy

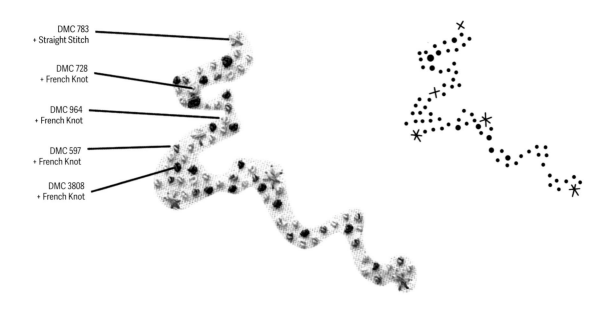

DMC 783
+ Straight Stitch

DMC 728
+ French Knot

DMC 964
+ French Knot

DMC 597
+ French Knot

DMC 3808
+ French Knot

Distant Spiral Galaxy

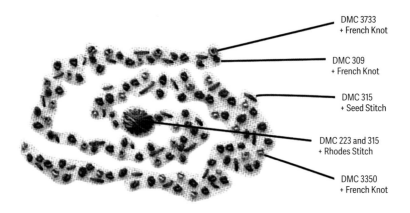

DMC 3733
+ French Knot

DMC 309
+ French Knot

DMC 315
+ Seed Stitch

DMC 223 and 315
+ Rhodes Stitch

DMC 3350
+ French Knot

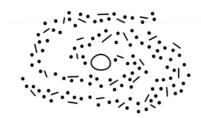

OTHER PLANTS

Branch with Acorns

DMC 319
+ Split Back Stitch

DMC 420 and 898
+ Split Back Stitch

DMC 898
+ Weave Stitch

DMC 898
+ Radial Satin Stitch

Eucalyptus

DMC 503
+ Leaf Stitch

DMC 501
+ Cretan Stitch

DMC 501
+ Stem Stitch

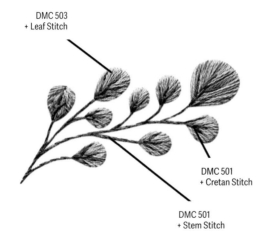

Venus Fly Trap

DMC 3348
+ Straight Stitch

DMC C321
+ Split Back Stitch

DMC 469
+ Long and Short
Satin Stitch

DMC 469
+ Split Back Stitch

DMC 581
+ Leaf Stitch

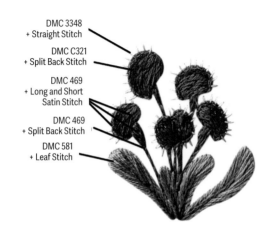

Palm Tree

DMC 937
+ Long and Short Satin Stitch

DMC 937
+ Leaf Stitch

DMC 898
+ Split Back Stitch

DMC 435
+ Reverse Chain Stitch

Olive Branch

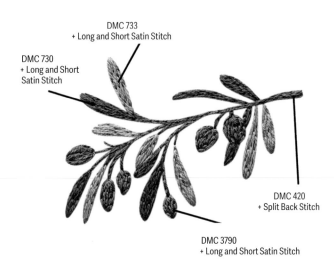

DMC 733
+ Long and Short Satin Stitch

DMC 730
+ Long and Short
Satin Stitch

DMC 420
+ Split Back Stitch

DMC 3790
+ Long and Short Satin Stitch

VEGETABLES

Corn

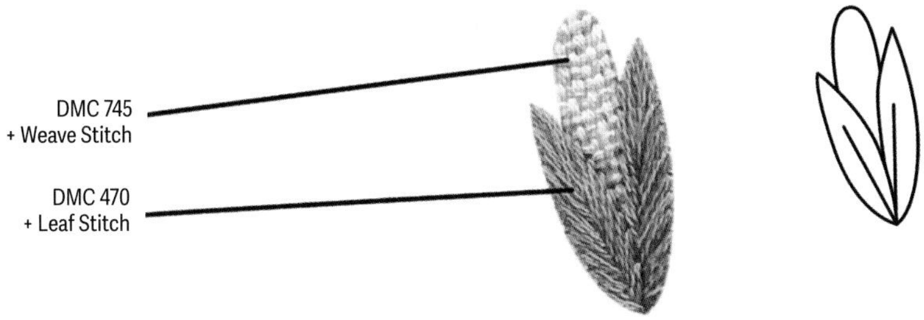

DMC 745
+ Weave Stitch

DMC 470
+ Leaf Stitch

Carrot

DMC 935
+ Fly Stitch

DMC 721
+ Long and Short Satin Stitch

DMC 900
+ Straight Stitch

Beet

DMC 895
+ Leaf Stitch

DMC 472
+ Fly Stitch

House of Embroidery
43 Flame A + Long
and Short Satin
Stitch

DMC 23
+ Split Back Stitch

Chili Pepper

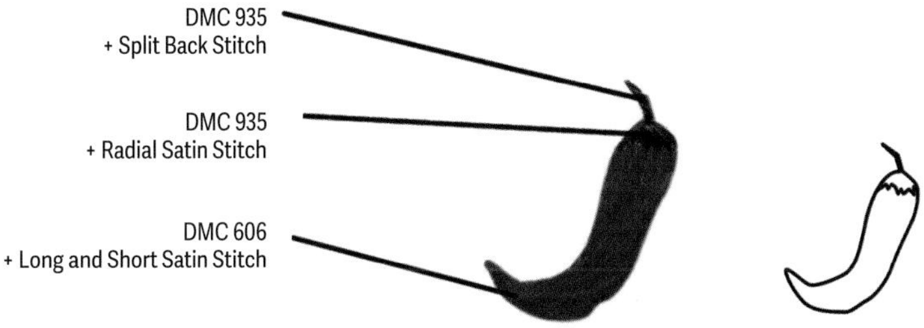

DMC 935
+ Split Back Stitch

DMC 935
+ Radial Satin Stitch

DMC 606
+ Long and Short Satin Stitch

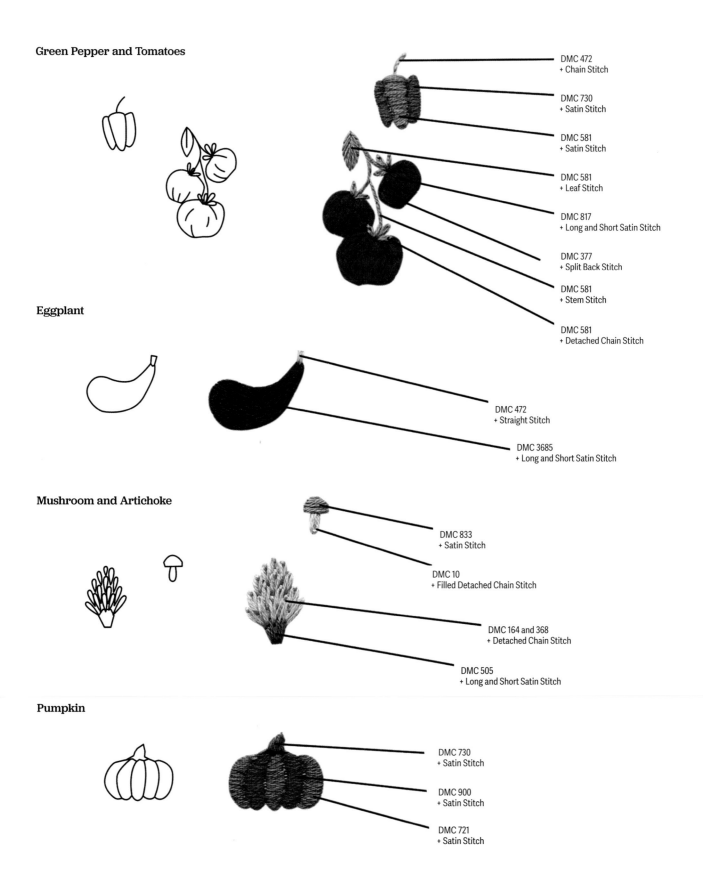

Green Pepper and Tomatoes

DMC 472
+ Chain Stitch

DMC 730
+ Satin Stitch

DMC 581
+ Satin Stitch

DMC 581
+ Leaf Stitch

DMC 817
+ Long and Short Satin Stitch

DMC 377
+ Split Back Stitch

DMC 581
+ Stem Stitch

DMC 581
+ Detached Chain Stitch

Eggplant

DMC 472
+ Straight Stitch

DMC 3685
+ Long and Short Satin Stitch

Mushroom and Artichoke

DMC 833
+ Satin Stitch

DMC 10
+ Filled Detached Chain Stitch

DMC 164 and 368
+ Detached Chain Stitch

DMC 505
+ Long and Short Satin Stitch

Pumpkin

DMC 730
+ Satin Stitch

DMC 900
+ Satin Stitch

DMC 721
+ Satin Stitch

Index

Note: Page numbers in *italics* indicate projects, patterns (in parentheses), and additional designs.

About Melissa

Melissa Galbraith is the fiber artist behind MCreativeJ. She was born and raised in the desert of Washington state where her mother instilled a love of making things by hand at an early age. Melissa shares her love of nature through whimsical and modern hand embroidery designs.

Melissa was reintroduced to hand embroidery after finding her desk job monotonous and needing a creative outlet. She loves that embroidery is like coloring with a needle and thread. Melissa found that many craft enthusiasts also wanted to learn how to embroider but were daunted by where to start. Thanks to this and a love of teaching, Melissa began to share her hand embroidery knowledge.

Melissa enjoys seeing makers fall in love with the needle arts, especially that magical "ah-ha" moment of learning something new. Explore even more hand embroidery with Melissa's first book, *How to Embroider Texture and Pattern*.